STOP OVERTHINKING + LETTING GO OF ANXIETY

2 IN 1- BOOST YOUR SELF-ESTEEM TO OVERCOME NEGATIVE THOUGHTS & ELIMINATE STRESS AND WORRY FROM YOUR LIFE

JOHN WARD

CONTENTS

STOP OVERTHINKING

LETTING GO OF ANXIETY

STOP OVERTHINKING

BOOST YOUR SELF-ESTEEM TO OVERCOME ALL NEGATIVE THOUGHTS AND STAY MOTIVATED

John Ward

John Ward

a result of the use of the information contained within this document, including, but not limited to, — errors, omissions, or inaccuracies.

"Don't wait. The time will never be just right."

Napoleon Hill

INTRODUCTION

Do you often get confused by your thoughts? Do you strive weekly with stress or anxiety about the things you need to fulfill? Do you just want to stop over-thinking life in general?

Now and then, we all experience negative thinking. But if you are still distracted by these feelings, then you can analyze carefully what you are thinking about and how your emotions affect your mental health.

This internal monologue is a regular part of your mentality. It's there all the time, night and day, continually telling you of the food you need to pick up, teasing you for skipping the birthday of your friend or making you feel nervous about current news (such as politics, the weather, or the current state of the economy). Such thoughts are your life's background noise, but you may not always be conscious of their relentless existence. Right now, take a second and pay close attention to your thinking. Try stopping your thoughts. It's tough, right? You can see how unbidden and sometimes unwanted they tend to flood in, one after another.

Some of your thoughts are obscure and unnecessary. "My arm is itching." "It looks like it's going to rain." Many of our emotions are distracting and pessimistic, on the other hand. "That guy is a jerk." "I screwed this project." "I am so culpable about what I said to Mama." Those thoughts clutter us, whether neutral, positive, or negative, just as your bedroom can be cluttered if you have too many personal belongings. Unfortunately, it is not so easy to clear up the mental clutter as it is to remove possession. You cannot "throwaway" a thought and wait for it to go down. Actually, like an endless Whack-a-Mole game, your negative thoughts will emerge as soon as you grope them down.

Now, envision in your mind a fully coordinated home – a home free from foreign, draining, and unnecessary objects that will agitate you. What if you can only surround yourself with ideas that lift, encourage, and ease you? Imagine your mind for a moment as a beautiful cloudless sky, and you have the freedom to choose what you want. If that bright mental sky is so ideal, why do we worry so much about random and unwanted thoughts with so few filters?

The brain has about 100 billion neurons, while the spinal cord comprises another billion. The cumulative number of interactions between neurons – the thinking cells – has been calculated to be 100 trillion. Our powerful brains actively process and evaluate all kinds of experiences in the form of thoughts. Thoughts shape what we see as truth.

We can regulate and direct our thoughts, but our thoughts sometimes feel as if they have their minds. They influence us and how we think. The idea is necessary to solve the problems, evaluate, determine, and prepare. Still, in the meantime, the mind roams like a wild monkey; it drags you through the thorns of negativity and rumination. Your daily inner conversation, right here and now, takes the focus away from you and from what is happening.

Absurdly, we believe that we have to think more or harder to 'work out' why we're not as glad or happy as we want to be. We seek to find assets, people, and interactions that can quench our desires and relieve our unhappiness. The more we think about our despair, the more we become despondent. Our minds make us anxious, hollow, and chaotic as we prepare for the future or look to the past for answers.

Indeed, almost every negative thought you have to do with the past or the future. It is normal to be stuck in a circuit of regrettable thoughts and concerns, even when feeling desperate to avoid the endless tape in your head.

This complex thinking or judging involves intense emotions. The more frightening, guilty, regrettable thoughts we have, the more stressed, worried, depressed, and frustrated we feel. The feelings often paralyze us with negative emotions, and those feelings deprive us of inner peace and joy.

Even if our emotions are the source of too much distress, you can't just stop thinking, right? You cannot shut your brain off at will or get rid of the mind chat and associated feelings that prevent you from truly enjoying life.

Now and then, we have natural inner calm and quiet moments. However, we seek to soothe mental debate more often by using too much food, alcohol, narcotics, work, sex, or exercise as self-medication. However, these are short-term solutions for noise muffling and pain relief. Our minds return to it soon enough, and the cycle continues.

Are we always bound to be accomplices of our "monkey minds"? Do we have to continue to battle our thoughts and let them weigh us down with guilt, remorse, and anxiety? Is there a way to have a pure, pain-free mind?

You may not always be able to keep your mind free from danger, but you may have ample effect on your outlook to boost your quality of life and overall happiness profoundly. Thinking may seem intuitive and uncontrollable, but many of our patterns of thought are regular and thoughtless.

While it seems integral to you and your feelings, you have a "conscious self" that can step in and control your thinking. You regulate your emotions even more than you think. When you start to adjust your mind, you open a path to the enormity of imagination, motivation, and ingenuity behind the untouched thoughts.

You will disable your thoughts and have more "space" in your mind to experience inner happiness and peace through practical habits and mindfulness practices. You will have the ability to determine what the essential thing in your life is, what no longer suits your goals, and how you want to live every day.

Many individuals overthink and over analyze every facet of their lives repeatedly, whether it is their careers, relationships, lack of success, or a relentless stream of stress. Almost all of these challenges in everyday life seem unavoidable.

Good habits such as meditation on consciousness, healthy relationships, and good sleep will take you to an environment where bad habits are lost. From unhealthy relationships to a cluttered living room, throwing away the reticence will give way to a whole new person, ready to face the challenges of life with a mind full of optimistic thoughts and concrete goals. I hope that you can understand your total capacity without feeling like overthinking every day, which means you can develop better habits. You can regain control.

This aim of the book is straightforward: I will educate you on the habits, actions, and thoughts that you can use to clean up the overthinking that could keep you from being more focused and conscious. Several books on this subject are available on the market; thank you once again for choosing this one. All attempts are made to guarantee that the knowledge is as useful as possible. Feel free to enjoy it.

1

MANAGE YOUR STORY

*O*verthinking is one of the most common mental conditions in the world, and unfortunately, it is also one of the most debilitating. You might think that it is no big deal, everybody gets lost in their thoughts sometimes, right?

Now, if you have any previous experience in falling into the almost endless spiraling pit of despair that is overthinking, then you know just how horrible it is. Overthinking can prevent you from enjoying the things that you used to love doing, like going to parties, walking in the park, or just meeting with friends. Overthinking can also negatively affect your performance at work, it makes you lose motivation, makes you procrastinate on your tasks, and thus ruining whatever chances of job progression you might have. Overthinking can also ruin your relationships; no one wants to be around a person who is always complaining, cranky, and has such a short temper so that you will have very few friends, and they might not be sticking around for much longer.

However, it seems like everything you do seems futile, it's as if there is always an insurmountable hurdle in front of you. Overthinking not only leaves you mentally drained, but it also makes you feel exhausted physically. It's like having an energy vampire latched permanently on your neck, and it is continuously feeding on what little mental and physical energy you have.

However, you should not lose hope just yet; there are plenty of ways that you can use to overcome your chronic overthinking problem. But first, you need to start with understanding the core problem; you need to know what overthinking is, and from there, you can start looking for the most viable solutions.

Everyone gets sucked into the rabbit hole of obsessive thoughts sometimes, and when it happens occasionally, then it is okay. However, when overthinking starts to consume your life, that is when it becomes a chronic mental problem.

Not everyone is prone to overthink, but some are more likely to suffer from it. For instance, people with a history of struggling with anxiety are almost always dealing with overthinking and its consequences daily. Overthinking is one of the triggers that cause stress in most people. Even if you do not have any history of mental health problems, if you consider yourself as a "problem solver" of sorts, then you are prone to overthinking. The thing you think as your most valuable asset, which is your analytical mind, can become your worst enemy when your overthinking is triggered.

If you are at a low point in your life where you have unusually high levels of uncertainty, it can trigger your overthinking disorder. Now that you have an idea of what overthinking is, the next thing that you need to know is the signs of overthinking to the lookout. Knowing the symptoms will inform you that you might need to be wary of the status of your mental health, maybe consider getting professional help. You can somehow gauge how deep into overthinking you are by identifying which symptoms have already manifested; if you find that you have signs of being a chronic overthinker, then you should probably consider getting professional help.

If you have trouble getting to sleep and you

cannot turn off your thoughts, even when you try, your thoughts start racing even faster when you try to stop them. All of these worries and doubts swirling in your head agitates you and prevents you from getting enough rest.

Overthinkers know the feeling of not getting enough sleep, almost too well actually. Insomnia happens because you have no control over your brain; you cannot shut off the chain of negative thoughts going through your mind at a hundred miles an hour. All of the things that worried you throughout the day come back just when you hit the sack, and you feel so wired that you cannot fall asleep.

If you are having difficulty calming your mind on your own, you can try different relaxing activities before you go to bed. There are plenty of things that might help you ease your mind just enough to let you get some sleep, like meditation, writing in a journal, adult coloring books, drawing, painting, reading a book, or even just having a pleasant conversation with a loved one. Do anything that can shift your attention away from the negative thoughts long enough for you to get some sleep.

Numerous medical researchers have discovered that most people suffering from overthinking disorders have turned to use recreational drugs, alcohol, overeating, or other ways to get a grip on their emotions somehow. Overthinkers feel the need to rely on external stimuli because they believe that their internal resources (aka their minds) are already compromised?

It is never a good idea to turn to try to treat yourself from overthinking. Odds are, you will still be overthinking afterward, and you have to deal with a different problem brought about by your self-medication.

If you are constantly feeling tired, you need to take action. Fatigue is your body's way of telling you to listen to it because there is something wrong going on; you should not ignore it and just hop from one activity to the next.

However, overthinking can also cause fatigue and exhaustion. Your mind is like a muscle; if you are continually burdening it with dozens of massive, negative thoughts all the time, and not even giving it some time to recover, it will get exhausted and cause you to burn out.

Back when humans were still living off the land, people did not have that many things to worry about, which means they do not have quite as many things to think about as well. In today's modern world, people lead complicated lives that require them to accomplish a lot of things in a short amount of time. In this fast-paced world, the need to slow down every once in a while is crucial for people's well-being. So, whenever you feel fatigued, or better yet, if you feel close to it, slow things down and figure out what your body, and your mind, needs before doing anything else.

Overthinkers have one major problem, and that is that they always feel that they need to be in control of everything. They plan out every aspect of their lives, some of them even go as far as planning up to the smallest detail. They feel that doing this is the only way they can feel safe, but it always seems to backfire at them because it is impossible to plan for everything that will happen in their lives.

Even so, they continue to plan out their futures, and they get anxious when unexpected things happen, and they always seem to be surprising things happening all the time. Overthinkers hate dealing with something that they do not have control over; they fear the unknown. When unexpected problems do surface, they cause them to sit and mull things over instead of taking immediate action to solve the unexpected issue. Numerous medical studies have shown that overthinking leads to making poor judgment calls, which is why over-thinking does not help.

When you catch yourself just before you start overthinking, try your best to bring your thoughts back to the present by taking deep breaths and thinking happy thoughts.

If you fancy yourself a perfectionist, and you often think about how awful you would feel if you were to fail somehow. This fear of failure can be so intense that it paralyzes you, and it keeps you from learning from your prior mistakes, which often lead to you repeating them.

Overthinkers often cannot accept failure, and they will do everything they can to avoid it. Ironically, they think that the only way not to fail is to do nothing at all. They mistakenly believe that to avoid failure, they should not put themselves in a position to fail at all, which also means they are not in the position to succeed as well.

If this sounds like you, remember that you are more than just your failures; no one could even remember the last time that you screwed up, it's just you. Also, keep in mind that it is impossible to escape failure, and you should never avoid it at all. For failure allows you to grow and evolve.

Instead of being excited about the things that you

are yet to experience, your anxiety and fear of what could go wrong paralyze you into doing nothing.

If you are afraid of what the future could bring, then your fear keeps you trapped inside your mind. Research shows that this fear of the future can be so crippling that sufferers tend to turn to drugs and alcohol so that they can tune out the negative thoughts that are clamoring inside their heads.

Tension headaches feel as if there is a thick rubber band wrapped around your temples, and it is slowly getting tighter. Aside from problems, you might also feel a sharp pain or stiffness in your neck. If you suffer from chronic tension headaches, it is a sign that you are overworking yourself, and you need a rest.

And by rest, it also includes rest from mental activities, like overthinking. Headaches are a sign that your body needs to take a break; this includes your mind. Even you might not notice it, but when you overthink, you are thinking of the same things over and over again.

Overthinkers usually have negative thought patterns that loop around themselves. To fight this, you need to break this loop by reinforcing positive thoughts. Take deep breaths, and focus your mind on every time your chest rises and falls, being mindful of the present will help you get rid of negative thoughts and the tension headache that came with them.

Stiff Joints and Muscle Pain- It might sound far-fetched, but overthinking can affect your entire body, not just your mind. And once your physical body is affected by your out of control negative thoughts, it will not be long until your emotional well-being gets hit too. Until you address and get rid of the under-lying issues that cause you to overthink, the body pains will continue. Overthinking might start in your mind, but its effects will gradually creep into the other parts of your body.

When you overthink, you will find it difficult living in the present moment and enjoy your life as it happens. Overthinking causes you to lose focus on the things happening around you; you are so engrossed at thinking about your problems. If your account gets bogged down by a ton of unnecessary thoughts, you are removing yourself from the present, and this can and will negatively affect your relationships.

You need to open yourself to the world around you; do not let yourself get too wrapped up in nega-tive thoughts. The only opinions that you should allow inside your mind are those that serve your well-being, ignore and forget about the ones that bring you down. There is so much beauty in life, and the opportunities for incredible experiences are unlimited. However, you can only appreciate them if you can manage to tune out the idle chatter in your mind and start listening to your heart instead.

DIFFERENT CAUSES OF OVERTHINKING

Again, there is nothing wrong about thinking about your problems so you can think of a solution for them, it becomes worrisome when you have a bad habit of twisting narratives around in your head until you can see every angle and side to it. Overthinking is not productive as it just makes you dwell over your problems; you are not looking for a solution for them, and you are only making yourself feel miserable

To find an effective way to break your over-thinking habit, you need to find out what caused it in the first place. Below are some of the more common reasons as to why people tend to overthink ;

If you are not self-confident, you tend to doubt every little thing that you say or do. When you hesitate, even a little, about the things that you want to do, you are letting uncertainty and fear creep into your mind, and it will be challenging to get them out of there. You can never really tell what your decisions will take you; even if you planned every little detail, the outcome will still not be what you hoped for (it could either be better or worse than what you expected).

It is only natural to worry when you encounter new and unfamiliar things and events. However, if you worry too much that you cannot even imagine a positive outcome, then it will trigger you to over-think. It is problematic because worry attracts even more problems, sometimes it creates ones out of thin air, which causes overthinking to go even deeper. Instead of mulling over how things could go wrong, it is better to entertain more positive thoughts, like how much better you would feel if a certain even turns in your favor.

Some people believe that they can protect them-selves from troubles whenever they overthink, but the truth is that overthinking is a trap that kills your progress. Overthinking and not doing anything to change the status quo might seem right, but stifling your development is never a good thing at all. Also, when you overthink, you are not staying in the same position, you are undoing whatever amount of progress you achieved thus far.

Many overthinkers became that way because

they cannot seem to get their minds off their problems no matter how hard they try.

Being a perfectionist is not necessarily a good thing. One could argue that being a perfectionist is not good at all. Most people who struggle with perfectionism are always anxious. They often wake up in the middle of the night, thinking of the things that they could have done better. Being a perfectionist causes overthinking because you are always trying to outdo yourself.

Reliance on quick fixes like with the advent of the internet also came a myriad of self-help videos, articles, and websites. The one thing that these resources promise is that they can help fix what ails you in a couple of easy steps. Of course, all of them are lying, but unfortunately, people usually have no other choice. However, many quick fixes do help, and that is the reason why it is problematic. Are you hungry? Just order a pizza or Chinese takeout using your phone. You do not like walking? Get yourself a car. Do you need to talk to your mother halfway across the country? Pick up your smartphone and start a video call. The modern world has so many quick fixes in place for almost every kind of problem that people might have. However, quick fixes just work most of the time, not every time. When a person's question remains unresolved for a few hours or even days, his mind automatically defaults to thinking that there must be something wrong, and this usually triggers overthinking.

For instance, if you are feeling upset for a couple of days, there must be some kind of quick fix for it. You think you need to quit your job, break up with your SO, stop talking to your parents; yes, these things might provide some form of cure for what ails you, but are these the correct choices, not necessarily. These options are Band-Aid fixes, not long-term solutions. And when these Band-Aid fixes eventually fail, people immediately fall into the spiral of overthinking.

When you feel stressed, the explanations that come to your mind are not the complete story. There are dozens of factors that might have contributed to your negative emotions, the things that you thought might be the reasons are just the tip of the iceberg. For instance, when you feel lethargic, you might think that it must be because you are unhappy with your job, or if you are having problems with your family, it does not even scrape your mind that you need more sleep because you are just skipping one hour of sleep. However, lack of sleep stacks up, and if you jump an hour of sleep every day for a week, your body will reflect all of the stresses that you have accumulated.

Western culture respects and encourages people to pursue their dreams. It can be positive, but when people believe that they can achieve their goals with little to no effort, that is when things go wrong. Most children grow up believing that they just need to be good little boys to get ahead in life, but then when they reach adulthood, the magic vanishes.

When a person first experiences the less than stellar world of the 9 to 5 office desk job, real relationship problems, and how incredibly bland and real healthy life is, they start to think of all the things that they might have done wrong for them to deserve their vanilla lives. When the gap between fantasy and reality becomes too high, it causes great sadness, which also causes them to give up on chasing their dreams.

For example, one person might think that there must be something wrong with the system because he did not get that promotion he worked hard to get, or why he is not feeling the effects of the economic boom that has been reported all over the news lately? It leads to even darker thoughts like maybe the reason he did not get that promotion was that he did not graduate from an Ivy League university. He starts blaming his parents for not paying for an Ivy League education. He also starts thinking that maybe it is his family that is holding him back from success, or perhaps the system at his work is rigged for him to fail. Or maybe, it is just that he is not as smart or as capable as his co-workers. All of these thoughts will start swirling around the person's head.

Although emotional awareness is still critical, you need to find a happy medium for it to become beneficial. The truth is that most men have ignored emotional awareness altogether, while most women have taken it a bit too far. It resulted in many women sitting and talking about their emotions. Still, rather than trying to fix their problems, this turns into an activity where they are just finding validation for their feelings. Not only is this kind of thing not helpful to your plight, but it can also be harmful and addictive. Rather than encouraging each other to take steps towards managing their emotions or solve their problems, they each stoke their fires, supporting themselves that their righteous indignation is justified and that there is nothing wrong with it.

Ignoring problems is terrible, but it also is taking self-awareness too far. People have become too introspective that even a twinge of sadness will trigger a rush of anxiety in them. Although some moods do hold messages, most of the time, their reasons are entirely inconsequential, like the horrible traffic on the way to work, or because you did not get enough coffee. People have become so hyper-vigilant about their emotions, and that alone is enough to fuel endless nights of overthinking.

2

LET GO OF THE PAST AND START
BUILDING THE FUTURE

*H*ave you at any point felt pushed, restless, or overpowered by life? We live in a bustling world. With messages and messages flying all around as you are venturing over your kids' toys and attempting to get the canine sustained while the nourishment on the table is getting cold, you most likely get a handle on worrying constantly.

Mindfulness will enable you to diminish your pressure and nervousness, limit the measure of time that you spend feeling overpowered, and help you value every little minute as it occurs. In a universe of confusion, mindfulness may very well be the stunt you have to figure out how to have the option to adapt to the frenzy.

Luckily, there is a straightforward propensity

you can use to quiet yourself down and acknowledge life more usually. It's called mindfulness. Mindfulness is the act of deliberately concentrating the majority of your consideration on the present minute and tolerating it without judgment.

ADVANTAGES OF MINDFULNESS

Mindfulness diminishes Uneasiness; research has discovered that mindfulness is particularly useful in reducing nervousness. Rehearsing mindfulness revamps your cerebrum so that you can refocus your consideration. As opposed to following a negative and stressing thought down a way of every single imaginable result, you can figure out how to see the truth about your contemplations and simply let them go.

Mindfulness also improves memory, focus, and execution on the job. Mindfulness is one of the not very many strategies that function as a remedy for mind-meandering and the negative impacts that losing focus may have on you.

Mindfulness gives relief from discomfort, around 100 million Americans experience the ill effects of ceaseless torment each day, yet 40% to 70% of these individuals are not accepting legitimate medicinal treatment. Numerous investigations have demonstrated that mindfulness contemplation can decrease agony without utilizing endogenous narcotic frameworks that are generally accepted to diminish pain during subjective based systems like mindfulness.

Oneself created a narcotic framework that has, as a rule, been suspected of as the focal piece of the mind for mitigating torment without the utilization of medications. This framework self-produces three narcotics, including beta-endorphin, the met-and Leu-enkephalins, and the dynorphins. These work together to lessen pain by rehearsing mindfulness.

One of the most well-known manifestations that join tension is rumination or overthinking. After you start to stress over something, your mind will clutch that firmly and make it difficult to give up. It is anything but difficult to get into an idea circle where you keep on replaying every single awful result possible. We as a whole realize this isn't valuable since stressing over something doesn't keep it from occurring.

One investigation demonstrated that individuals who were new to mindfulness and started to rehearse it during a retreat had the option to give fewer indications of rumination and uneasiness than the control gathering.

Another advantage of mindfulness is in its impacts on the amygdala, which is the cerebrum's enthusiastic preparing focus. The unwinding reaction that your body needs to mindfulness reflection is a remarkable inverse of the pressure reaction. This unwinding reaction attempts to ease many pressures related to medical problems, for example, agony, wretchedness, and hypertension. Rest issues are regularly attached to these illnesses.

One investigation of more established grown-ups affirms that mindfulness contemplation can help in getting a decent night's rest. As indicated by this examination, mindfulness reflection can expand the unwinding reaction through its capacity to develop attentional components that confer command over the autonomic sensory system.

Mindfulness advances mental Wellbeing-Specialists have discovered that IBMT (integrative body-mind preparing) starts positive auxiliary changes in the cerebrum that could help secure against cerebral infection. The act of this strategy helps support productivity in a piece of the cerebrum that enables individuals to direct behavior.

Mindfulness advances intellectual adaptability; one examination proposes that not exclusively will mindfulness help individuals become less receptive;

it may likewise give individuals progressively mental flexibility. Individuals who practice mindfulness seem, by all accounts, to be ready also to rehearse self-perception, which consequently withdraws the pathways made in the cerebrum from earlier learning and permits data that is going on right now.

Mindfulness is not some practice limited to monks who have taken a vow of silence. It is the type of training that virtually anyone can do, at any time, and anywhere.

So, here are some additional strategies to implement mindfulness in your everyday life:

Sit with your experience at the point when you center on being careful, rehearsing mindfulness through concentrating on your body, psyche, and soul will enable you to turn out to be all the more dominant. The more you do this, the more you shut out the sense of self and the better you will feel in all pieces of yourself. Tune in for sounds that are close by or even far away. Output your body to get a feeling of what is loose and what is holding strain. If you have a tingle, see the tingle, however, don't attempt to transform it. Simply travel through it. It is an excellent practice for simply being careful without trying to take care of business.

Once in a while, life is awkward, like a tingle.

Sitting with the experience will enable you to see that things go back and forth. Nervousness can sneak up in your gut, or you may encounter a snugness in your throat while you reflect.

Mindfulness doesn't mean getting to be associated with the show of the psyche. It's tied in with seeing how the mind and body are reacting with full acknowledgment.

The touchy individual in you who has had numerous encounters will feel apprehensive, destitute, and desirous every once in a while. It is the mind and the conscience affecting everything. You are the caring person; you are the inhabiting being who knows.

To take advantage of the piece of you that sits looking out for this human experience, you simply need to remain completely focused. All of what I'm stating may appear to be exceptionally perplexing for some who have never polished mindfulness. It just requires some investment of not responding, and instead of watching your experience to comprehend the procedure, I'm discussing.

Reflection is an incredible practice for minutes that bring awkward feelings.

Make proper acquaintance with the one in your brain. Just inside, make a proper acquaintance. Who makes an appropriate acquaintance, and who hears him? It's you who's talking, and it's you who's tuning in.

The ideal approach to turn out to be free from the steady prattle that is bolstering your horrendous thoughts is to step back. Take a gander at it dispassionately. Musings are only an object of the psyche, something that should drift by and not be clutched or dismissed.

As you're careful and watch the voice, you'll start to see that the more significant part of what it says has next to no significance. It complains about the past and utilizes old encounters to attempt to control the present and future meetings. It causes a wide range of issues in your life.

If you need to turn out to be free from your brain, you must be careful enough to observe indeed what's happening up there. At the point when you discover that a lot of your activities originate from some nonsensical voice that wants comfort, you can start to settle on different choices.

All in all, mindfulness can mend numerous things, yet how would we accomplish it? One of the pathways to calm the psyche and go within ourselves is through contemplation.

Contemplation isn't tricky, but then its effortlessness threatens many. It is because your self-image wouldn't like to be calmed. It reveals to you that you're excessively occupied, that reflection is inconsequential, and that it's overly unusual and otherworldly for you.

What's truly going on is that the self-image is terrified of ending up calm. Backing off and going in methods, there's the capability of standing up to awkward sentiments. You gave your sense of self the activity of keeping away from distress or saw peril.

At the point when we ponder, there is an incredible danger of running into past torment.

Mindfulness, through your contemplation, enables you to at long last manage old injuries, so you don't need to live with them any longer. That implies that they never again have power over you.

To develop mindfulness, you'll need to invest significant energy consistently, yet this shouldn't be a task. The mind will prattle and reveal to you it's exhausted. Simply continue watching the objects of musings and emotions traveling through you.

The more you practice, the more you'll anticipate having that uninterrupted alone time. Consider it daily in the spa or getting a back rub. When you get into it, that focused inclination makes you feel as loose as 40 minutes in a sauna. While you'll start to experience benefits practically immediately, the more you practice mindfulness, the more unique the advantages will be in both the Buddhist ways of thinking and present-day psychotherapy. There is a wide range of approaches to reflect as well, so don't sit in lotus posture and consume those incense sticks at this time. Reflection is the umbrella for mending, and inside your contemplations, you can accomplish numerous things for the body, psyche, and soul.

Mindfulness contemplation isn't tied in with changing or modifying yourself in any capacity. It's tied in with getting to be mindful of what your identity is. As you sit peacefully, things will come up. As you search inside yourself, recollections may come up as if they are a motion picture on a screen. If you remain in the seat of cognizance without getting sucked in, you can become familiar with a great deal. You'll know if you get sucked in because you won't let pictures go. You'll get genuinely included, and pressure will begin to develop.

Buddha said that the wellspring of your enduring is attempting to flee from your direct experience. Remaining in a lovely minute from your past is equivalent to pieces of torment. Clutching things keeps you before, and it's mostly not beneficial for your mind.

COACHING TIPS:

- 1. To reduce and avoid overthinking, use validated techniques. Surprisingly, one of the simplest is the most effective. Distract yourself. Choose to turn your mind literally into something else, ideally absorbing and enjoying exciting and optimistic thoughts. Instead, many people find a stop sign and say either in their heads the word, "stop!" whenever the situation loudly requires it to be ruminated.

- 2. Offer yourselves to excellence. Learn to laugh at errors and challenges, welcome human error, and find irony and fun in it as it happens. Suppose people's lives are full and there are likely alternative explanations for what could be seen as a snub or power play otherwise. Realize that it's not about you most of the time.

- 3. Prevent causes. Keep away and limit your time to people or situations that lead you to feel depressed and think again as much as possible. Identify who and what and how your sensitivity to these stimuli can be reduced.

- 4. Go to "stream." Find areas of your life where you get so lost, whether it is playing the piano, shooting hoops, reading, walking, or kayaking. Schedule the stream times for events in your life every week, if possible, daily.

- 5. Learn, learn, practice, and practice! Ultimately, pick some of these tips, training, and practice. Study shows that it takes a lot of practice to "hardwire" a new habit, so be patient with yourself and just continue to use your unique strategies to turn your mind in an overthinking way. You should be both happier and more productive with time and practice.

You can practice a relaxation method like progressive muscle relaxation because people who display generalized anxiety often have high levels of responsiveness. Take up short-term activities that are captivating and enjoyable to take your mind off certain things and distract them from specific negative thoughts. These could be activities that have been useful in the past. An exercise is a vital tool for managing worry. When you exercise, brain chemicals are released that counteract low moods, fear, and anxiety. The practice also acts as a distraction from problems and reduces nervousness. Exercise at least once a day for half an hour, with cardio, exercises at least three days a week.

Incorporate organized problem-solving strategies to handle stressors that contribute to your worry. Everyone has problems and challenges in their lives, but they are more visible and challenging to handle if you always get worried. A useful strategy to combat this is training in organized problem-solving. Efficient problem-solving techniques minimize, reduce, control, and even prevent worrying in our daily lives.

Avoid activities and situations that foster anxiety by confronting your fears and facing them directly but gradually. For instance, you could place them in a hierarchy, depending on which step you fear the most. These fears could be: Arriving late for a meeting, Not checking your mobile phone for one hour, Going grocery shopping without a shopping list, Planning a birthday party, and accepting an invitation without checking with your calendar.

Well, as soon a person has been able to identify

and question his or her negative thoughts, then the next line of action is shifting attention away from the negative thoughts. Cognitive Behavioural Therapy assists in identifying and challenging these assumptions and helping individuals to develop alternative beliefs that are healthier and better for their well-being. Experiences have shown that mindfulness-based interventions will also aid you to remain focused.

Adopt Emotion Regulation and Mindfulness, recent studies have suggested that worry may present itself as a way of doing away with emotional processing. Involve yourself in what is called emotion-regulation strategies and mindfulness skills, as these will boost the form and manner in which you identify and experience underlying emotions.

Do away with the use of medications that will sedate you. Don't binge to relieve your anxiety. They may provide temporary relief from stress, but frankly, it will come back later. Instead of doing these, set up a time to consult a specialist or go for CBT if symptoms occur for longer than three months regardless of the above measures.

3

BECOME A PERSON OF ACTION

*F*inding a balance between thinking and acting is a challenge for many people, especially for those who are independent. How much time should you spend thinking versus acting? We hear advice all the time about creating plans for action, which implies that a careful collection of thoughts should govern all work. But then there is also the pressure to "Do It Now," which requires immediate action all the time and especially in these changing times of today.

How to know when to think vs. when to act What is the balance point between impulsive action and retardant thinking? It seems clear that the right balance of both required, especially when you have your own business. However, the problem tends to yield to a small change in perspective. One that allows us to see that acting and thinking are much more similar than different. One of them is a physical action; the other is a mental action. I believe that the imbalance between thought and action is itself a symptom of a much larger internal inconsistency. You think you should achieve this balance when both things take you on different paths. You believe in one direction, but you act in another. It is easy to fall into a state of imbalance when you achieve a small change of perspective in your thoughts, but the inertia that you carry still guides your actions. In this way, you continue working under your old paradigms, but thinking within the framework of some new ones. It is only there, where you realize that thinking and acting are different things in themselves. You get results from both, but each takes you on slightly different routes, so it's easy to ask yourself which of the two paths is correct.

Overthinking might not seem so awful because thinking is excellent. Isn't that so? In any case, overthinking can cause issues. When you overthink, your decisions get overcast, and your pressure gets raised. You invest an excessive amount of energy in the negative, and it can wind up hard to act on it. On the off chance that this feels like a natural area to you, here are some straightforward plans to liberate your-self from overthinking. Occupy yourself into Joy, and once in a while, it is useful to have an approach to divert yourself with upbeat, positive, solid choices. Things like mediation, moving, working out, learning an instrument, weaving, drawing, and painting can separate you from the issues enough to close down the over-analysis.

You cannot have a remorseful idea and a thankful idea simultaneously, so why not invest the energy decidedly? Each morning and each night, make a rundown of what you are appreciative of. Get an appreciation for amigo and trade records, so you have an observer of the beneficial things that are around you.

Overthinking is something that can transpire. In any case, if you have an incredible framework for managing it, you can, at any rate, avert a portion of the negative, on edge, distressing thinking and trans-form it into something helpful, gainful, and successful.

It is, in every case, simple to make things more significant and more harmful than they should be. Whenever you find yourself preparing a specific mountain out of a molehill, ask yourself the amount it will matter in five years. Or on the other hand, so far as that is concerned, one month from now. Only this essential inquiry, switching up the period, can help shut down overthinking.

Before you can start to address or adapt to your propensity for overthinking, you have to figure out how to know about it when it is occurring. Whenever you wind up questioning or feeling pushed or restless, advance back and take a gander at the circumstance and how you are reacting, at that time of mindfulness is the seed of the change you need to make.

Confidence is a position of a riddle, where we discover the boldness to have faith in what we cannot see, and the solidarity to relinquish our dread of vulnerability. Each time I go into contemplation, it is a demonstration of trust, of squeezing into terror and drawing nearer to reality. Organize your shoulders and your feet level against the floor. Spot your hands over your kidneys (at your back under your lower ribs). Picture them and the little adrenal organs over them in your psyche. Furthermore, that is the place qigong contemplation steps in. By rehashing positive musings, you can make and fortify neural pathways, and clear up the kidneys, to assist you with more noteworthy authority over your feelings.

After a couple of breath cycles, lean forward a

little as you breathe in, catch your hands beneath your knees, open your eyes, and envision breathing out dread, making a "choo" sound. Close your eyes, grin, and breathe in your stomach out envisioning dull blue light and harmony encompassing your kidneys and adrenal organs. Breath out by driving your stomach back in.

Similarly, as with any feeling, contemplation can help balance out us, notwithstanding trepidation, to enable us to comprehend it all the more unmistakably. As the day progresses,

you can allow yourself to meet dread in an increasingly positive manner with the intensity of reflection. Check-in with your feelings consistently. At whatever point you feel dreadful, let the inclination remain. Rather than running, adopt a full breath and strategy your contemplations of fear and stress with neighborliness and interest. Be thoughtful to yourself in dread, as you would for a confided in a companion. If you have the opportunity and space, plunk down and inhale into your terror for ten breath cycles. Dread is stating that this is the ideal time to have the option to do what you're attempting to do. Your body is setting you up to have a positive result. When you can truly comprehend that dread is a feeling like some other feeling, you can figure out how to oversee it. And afterward, you can accomplish things that the vast majority consider to be exceptional. To beat my dread of statutes, I have grasped the fear, taking a lead shake climbing class where I need to move to the highest point of the divider and free fall mostly down the divider before being securely gotten with a rope. Through training, receptiveness, and cheering companions and teachers, I have figured out how to inhale through the dread and let go again and again.

Regardless of whether you are apprehensive because you have flopped previously, or you are frightful of attempting or over-generalizing some other disappointment, recall that since things did not work out, that does not imply that must be the result inevitably. Keep in mind, and each open door is a fresh start, a spot to begin once more. The dread that grounds overthinking is regularly situated in inclination that you are not sufficient or not savvy enough or persevering enough or devoted enough. When you have put forth a strong effort, acknowledge it in that capacity, and realize that, while achievement may depend to a limited extent on certain things you cannot control, you have done what you could do.

Give yourself a limit. Set a clock for five minutes and give yourself that opportunity to think, stress, and dissect. When the timer goes off, go through 5 minutes with a pen and paper, recording every one of the things that are stressing you, focusing on you, or giving you nervousness. Allow it to tear. At the point when the 5 minutes is up, toss the paper out and proceed onward ideally to something fun.

Try not to consider what can turn out badly, yet what can go right-As a rule, overthinking is brought about by a solitary feeling: dread. When you center around all the negative things that may occur, it is anything but difficult to end up deadened. If you feel that you might be going down this road for any reason, then stop yourself. Picture every one of the things that can go right and keep those contemplations present and in advance.

Nobody can foresee the future; the total of what we have is present. If you spend the current minute stressing over the future, you deny yourself of your time now. Investing energy, later on, is just not beneficial. Invest that energy instead on things that give you satisfaction.

For us all who are hanging tight for flawlessness, we can quit holding up this moment. Being driven is incredible, yet going for flawlessness is ridiculous, illogical, and crippling. The minute you begin thinking, "This should be immaculate" is simply the minute you have to remind yourself, "Sitting tight for impeccable is never as brilliant as gaining ground."

Life consists of thousands of moments, but we only live one moment at a time. When we start changing this moment, we start changing our lives. Are you somebody who likes to overthink things? Trinidad Hunt. Nonetheless, what exactly is overthinking? According to psychologists, who have done extensive research in the field, rethinking is' too much, needlessly and passively thinking; always pondering the significance, triggers and consequences of your personality, your emotions and particularly your problems.' It can mean lying awake at night thinking, "This economy is terrible; my savings are not worth it; I will probably lose my job and, I will never be able to send my kids back to college." Or it can mean thinking about how unattractive your delicate and wispy hair is several times over the day. Three days ago. Is he mad about something? Is he punishing me? Am I too insignificant to bother?" Someone who spends a lot of time wondering why a friend or boss hasn't made eye contact or spoken to them in a room, sits down to feel bad and then doesn't think it's worth putting in the effort or taking risks involved in top performance. Most people believe that if they feel disappointed or depressed by certain things, it will encourage them to think deeply and examine the situation to sort it out. When we look at science, the truth is just the opposite. Instead of being supportive, constant ruminations about possible adverse incidents tend to make people worse. Yes, according to Lyubomirsky, there is widespread and significant evidence that thinking about a painful or troubling situation is terrible for us over and over (also called "rumination"). It can be so harmful that it prevents us from taking significant proactive steps to improve the condition and can lead to an increasing deterioration of attitude, cynical distortion of reality, and even clinical depression in those who are vulnerable. Life and the world around you are all full of problems, from minor annoyances, mistakes, and imperfections to major tragic events and frightening threats and possibilities. It does not make us more stable or somehow less vulnerable to any of these innovations. It makes us feel worse and makes us less likely to take constructive action to improve our attitude or to reverse those changes. How can your job, your personal goals, your family, and your relationships be overlooked? It can make you feel so pessimistic that you avoid taking risks, reaching out to others, and making significant efforts to be successful. It can make it hard and even frustrating to be around for those who most matter to you. Ultimately, rethinking, with its forecasts of inevitable failure and terrible consequences, can drain the optimism required to work hard, speak up, and spread good thoughts.

Revisiting your daily objectives holds a lot of weight in today's society, where people flounder and don't know what they truly want. Instead, they struggle to make ends meet, have to plan to get themselves out of sticky situations and find themselves more lost than ever. You might be buried in your to-do list and don't know how to get out of it. The best approach is to stick to your goals.

Immediately when you get up in the morning, write down your daily goals, as well as the tasks and activities you hope to accomplish in your future. You will become motivated to do all the things you set out to do, and then you will be sure of a better future.

You might be thinking, "Where am I going to be in five or ten years?" To answer this vital question, you need to examine what you are doing at this moment. How are you tackling your goals daily? How are you growing or learning? Are you approaching your goals from a progressive and positive perspective?

Many people think that events are going to shift

their future in the direction where they want to go. They mystically believe that some miracle is going to make their dreams come true. However, this is not a reality. Instead, your life will shift in new directions only when you decide you want to alter it. How are you acting to ensure that you can get out of your unpleasant circumstances? You have to consider all the implications of your daily actions.

Sometimes, you have to look forward and then look backward. Use the future anterior tense in this case. After I achieve my dreams, I will have done _____ every day. For example, I will have worked out more, read more, and gotten a lot of tasks done.

Think as though you have already achieved your dreams and then work backward. You will then find that success is around the corner.

Hard times are sure to strike you, and you have to be ready for them. You need to be proactive in the process. Don't let it catch you by surprise. You must have a plan in place that you will turn to if and when you go through trials and tribulations. As you write out your goals, you need to stick to them in every situation. When you encounter the rocks on life's path, you need to know precisely how you will respond.

4

STOP YOUR THOUGHTS IN THE MOMENT AND PRACTICE BEING PRESENT

*M*ost people suffering from chronic stress, anxiety, and panic disorders develop an unhealthy habit, which makes them feel more anxious, less comfortable, and less satisfied. For some, their unhealthy habits – small exercise, irregular sleep, running food – had been in play long before the anxiety disorder developed, and perhaps one of the reasons why they were first out of touch with anxiety. For others, their unhealthy habits started as they grew anxiety issues. You skipped the workout because you were too afraid and afraid to have a quick walk or a morning run into your day. They often eat on the run or eat fat and sugar when they are anxious or down. They have fast food. Whether your dysfunctional patterns have come before or after your nervous problems, you need to fix these unhealthy environments.

You can learn in this chapter about the vital part of the management of your anxiety and the full recovery from your excessive anxiety and anxiety disorder by exercise, and sleep.

How Regular Exercise, Good Nutrition, And Adequate Sleep Can Help.

You may have problems doing the things you know may help if you are having excessive anxiety or an anxiety disorder. If you take 30 minutes to walk around the block, you can interrupt your workout exercises, because you too are upset that an important deadline is missed. You can save lunch and eat junk food at your office because in the morning you were too busy packing lunch. And what's the difference? You don't know anyway what you drank because you didn't eat attentively. You can remain exhausted as you try to fit another thing in your day, then lie awake thinking that because of tiredness and poor sleep, you might no longer be your best the next day. Yet regular exercise, proper nutrition, and good sleep are vital elements of any scheme that can fully recover from chronic stress and anxiety disorder.

You'll better protect yourself from stress and experience fewer symptoms of too much anxiety through regular exercise. Exercise can not only reduce the strength of your stress response over time, but you will also feel less nervous for some time after exercising every day. You can shield yourself from unnecessary spikes of blood sugar levels with proper nutrition, which can increase your depression and worsen your mood. Adequate nutrition also removes your depression aggravating compounds such as caffeine, which can relax the body and spirit, or even boost your health, in your diet. You will protect yourself from fluctuations in your anxious reaction and mood, if you're not well-rested, with sufficient sleep. They will also look out against the extra stress and worry that many people begin to think about and worry about the consequences of rest.

GETTING AND STAYING IN SHAPE

Daily exercise is good for almost everybody, but it is particularly crucial if you have an anxiety disorder. Several studies have shown that people with regular exercise have fewer effects of anxiety and depression and lower rates. Also, the practice seems to protect people against anxiety and mood conditions. Regular exercise has another advantage. After your workout, you will feel less anxious and feel more comfortable.

In other words, although it may take weeks for you to feel less nervous about doing this significantly, you will not feel more anxious after the workout, and each day you get this advantage. In reality, the more you are involved, the more so are the immediate effects of exercise.

Your willingness to do this will affect how you practice and what amount and type of exercise you choose. Here are a few tips to help you develop an exercise routine that you will not only love but also like to do regularly.

Fit an exercise routine into your life instead of fitting your life into an exercise routine. They do the best practice-regularly. In other words, regular people have chosen a workout routine that works for them in their lives. When you know, for example, that swimming would be right for you, but it is challenging to do a tour of the pool (the journey back and forth, the bathing, the shower). So as long as you believe you "can" dive, swimming in some other way might make more sense. Maybe it's better to just walk out of the door to stretch or jog around, or you can go and get out of work by car. For example, you can swim if you can concentrate on it, but it may be a mistake to build an exercise schedule around an unusual activity. Therefore, when you face the pressure of turning your current life into one particular practice, you can enjoy the event less.

Enjoy yourself. Regardless of how you prefer to exercise, you will have less fun some days than other days. If you go, you will one day feel like pushing a fridge down the sidewalk, and you must drive to complete the race. You will have a glorious time on other days. You'll be the same size, but you'll feel lighter and faster, and you will have an incredible sense of well-being. So running is a beautiful thing – shift your arms and legs, balance, let your body do what it's meant to do minute by minute. Nevertheless, even in days where the workout schedule is not especially enjoyed, you will still enjoy the training itself; after and after exercise, you will feel less stressed. It can help you remember when you roll the cooler down the sidewalk behind you.

If you pick a kind of workout you like: tennis, running, and salsa dancing, you will enjoy exercising more. Exercise does not mean to run a mile or to swim for 50 laps before work. When it suits your skills and interests, aerobic training can be enjoyable. You can do any physical activity that your heart pumps. You might want to choose three or five things that you may want to keep your exercise healthy and fun if you never enjoyed it. Then decide when you can participate in these things on your daily sched-ule. Be as rational as you can. A 30-minute walk in the countryside after school, when you have to get your child to tutor or make a family dinner, can be hard for your day; shooting your child in the court-yard with hoops for 30 minutes after tutoring, but it could be suitable for your day before lunch.

Reward yourself. There is an excellent reward for the immediate benefits of running–reduced depression and more well-being. Track your workout routine and use this immediate advantage to repay you, including the decline in your stress response after training. You can also track the workout routine's enjoyment.

Find other ways to make a difference while exer-cising. Take a warm shower after the exercise for a few minutes. Good job, say to yourself; believe it. Smile, after use, Any work is a good job. Note, after some days of exercising, you will feel great, and not so big some days. Award yourself. Use the reward plan of dot-to-dot. Draw an image that is an excellent reward using a sheet of graph paper and draw it. Click on a picture of your new phone or on a palm tree for that weekend, for example, to make a picture from a magazine. Put the cut-out image on the paper graph and trace it slightly. Now draw a dot where the image touches a line on the paper. Whenever you exercise, darken one point and connect with the one that you just darkened to the previous darkened dot. Take a small bonus per third or fourth point you obscure; a manicure, a movie, an hour to do correctly, and just what you want to. When you attach all the points, award yourself the big prize.

Develop the habit of exercising. There are major customary things, like "thank you" if someone does something good for you or gives you a free ride to work in the morning even when you want to go to the beach. Yet customs can also cause problems. Take into account the anxious patterns or habits in your fearful response. How useful are these customs? Developing an exercise habit will assist you in changing the harmless habits and trends in your anxious reaction. A definite pattern of exercise may increase the flexibility and emotional response to objects, activities, and situations of your thinking and actions. But they can be as hard to construct as they can break, as can many habits. Try to follow R four: Routine, Reward, Remind, and Relax to create a practice habit.

Do you think about where your life is headed now? Do you plan for the future only to see your plans turn to nothing? You're not alone. Self-discipline is a tireless effort, and it does not come easy to most people. Have you ever made a promise to yourself on New Year's Eve that you won't smoke another cigarette or have another drink, only to see your resolution come under fire the next day? We all find ourselves struggling to make and keep our New Year's resolutions because we simply don't have the self-discipline and willpower necessary to keep these promises to ourselves.

Because it is hard to keep our resolutions, we should consider the different ways we can make self-discipline last in our lives. There are a variety of ways we can limit our consumption of sugar, cut down on cigarettes, eliminate excessive binge-watching of TV and movies, etc. Let's look at some ways you can stop procrastinating on building self-discipline and start fresh today.

What we need to recognize is that the power lies within ourselves to change things. We should take full responsibility for our actions and do the things that will get us on the entire road to recovery. Recognize that no one is going to make you successful in your life. Only you can do this for yourself. You should be fully responsible for your finances, happiness, success, and health. Once you leave behind the influences of family, including relying on mom and dad or other people in your life and begin to make choices for yourself, you become fully responsible for what happens in your life and your preferences.

It is you who chooses the job you work at, the people you live with, your significant other, and how much you work out every day. You have to decide to use your time wisely. The decisions you make every day will have temporary and long-term consequences.

To improve your quality of life, you should become an expert in decision-making. Don't blame other people for your poor decision. It makes you look weak and irresponsible. Take responsibility for all the choices you make in your life. Although you may not be in control of all situations, you can control how you will respond: either maturely or foolishly.

Brian Tracy has talked about the fact that the biggest hindrance to a person's success is the easy way out. By choosing things that are easy for you, it will become impossible to achieve success and breakthroughs in the areas of your life that you want to change. Every battle we fight requires us to sacrifice something, and every success we can have has to have something that we give. However, most people never do this because they are lazy and unmotivated.

If you avoid doing the necessary things, you will avoid growing as a person, and you will also lose a sense of self-confidence. When you project yourself in a negative light, your reputation will paint you as a lazy and pitiful person.

If you want to achieve self-discipline, it will require a vision of where you want to be, a game plan, and repeated patterns that continue to work. It will be simple to write up your goals and determine what steps you need to take. But the last part is going to be the hardest because it requires your entire industry to achieve.

Do the things that are necessary and difficult because those things are going to matter more than the easy and fun aspects of life. You sometimes have to bust your butt to get ahead, and this is a crucial step to take. For you to achieve a high level of self-discipline, you should bear in mind that there is a bigger picture out there. You have to recall the reasoning for your actions and keep your promises, although the going will become tough. Bear in mind. However, that hard work does not have to be futile, like Sisyphus rolling the stone up the hill. But with your objectives in mind, you will be able to fulfill your goals.

By making a contract with yourself, you will

ensure that you don't break it, and you can make it a reality. Although you might not be able to achieve your goal immediately, it will happen eventually.

Because nothing in life is going to be simple, you must sacrifice your sleep, time, and effort to achieve the things you want. Undoubtedly, you will encounter situations that will set you back. As you edge closer to your success, you will also meet more adversity and testing than before. But as you pass each life test, you will find that your resolve becomes more firm and secure. Moreover, you become more resilient and bulletproof. Think of all the arrows coming out at you, but you're able to dodge them and become more influential in the process. Your shield of honor and motivation will be what get you through the difficult times.

Success has to be hard because it makes you stand out from the crowd. If it were easy, anyone could accomplish it, and then it wouldn't exist. It would be the easy road that leads to destruction. However, success is a road that you need to take, and it is the narrow way that not everyone is going to be able to achieve. The majority of people will fail to see it materialize.

Many people surrender to their fear and anxiety before they achieve their goals. They cross a mile-marker, and then they need to push themselves to run the race or the marathon, only to have their hope dashed by an obstacle that comes their way.

The moral of the story is that you need never to give up. Don't give in to the fear that may crush you. Instead, face your fear and own up to the fact that life is hard. Face everything with a mindset that you can do it because you're worth it.

Practice gratitude, and make it a daily habit. It is one of the secrets of highly successful people; they have made practicing gratitude a part of their daily habits. It is an effortless task, and it entails that you notice every last good thing that happens to you every day. When you are done seeing the little details and the God things that have happened to you that day, write them down in a journal. This practice may be hard to keep up at first, but the aim is to get you to a place where you develop the eye that has been trained to see the right things and a reason to be grateful in every situation.

Whenever you are about to be overwhelmed by negative thoughts and the reality of the fact that life can be harmful, commit to fixating on thinking good thoughts. There has to be a silver lining to hold on to amid every storm, right? That is the same thing you do once you carry out this exercise. Every time you are about to be overwhelmed by something negative, pick out memory from your past and fixate on it. Let it be a memory that puts a smile on your face. Doing this will make sure that you are not overwhelmed by the feelings of weakness that come with thinking of negativity all the time.

Talk to someone. Sometimes, it may not be easy for you to achieve this all by yourself, and that is why it becomes vital for you to talk to someone. It may be a therapist or a trusted person who can help you out of the dark place, but the goal is to make sure that you do not sink into the pool of feeling bad when you can reach out to someone who can offer some sort of help to you. The result of this is that they hardly ever get to live in the present, and if you do not live in the present, then you do not have any hopes of achieving anything remarkable.

Goal-oriented people know that if they must achieve the things that they have set out to make, they owe it to themselves and to the people around them to live in the moment. They know this because they have been in the place where they stressed out about everything that was not the present, and they were able to tell after a long time that all they did was just waste their time. Here are a few reasons why you must live in the present.

Have this knowledge and be very clear about it; the past is in the past for a reason. There is nothing you can do to change it, and the only definite way to take a look at your history is to try and draw lessons from it that you can apply to the present to change the future.

For example, a man who has just been relieved of his job can choose to sit down all day and lament the fact that he was sacked, or he can decide to take a look at his contribution to the whole thing. It could have been that he was not as productive as he should have been, or that there were other reasons why he was relieved. In place of crying incessantly about the job he lost, he can take it upon himself to improve his skill set so that he can become an employable worker in another firm, and be more productive at his new job. It is the mindset you must adopt if you are going to start living in the present.

There are times it helps for you to get off your mind from the big goal and focus on the small wins that will get you to your big goal. Let's face it; it is a great thing to feel that rush of dopamine and feel happy at the thoughts that you have a big goal to meet. However, it can be daunting just to keep an eye on the target. So instead of looking at the big goal and getting discouraged at how impossible it seems, focus more on the little wins that will culminate in the big goal. Instead of stressing out about how far your Ph.D. appears to be from you, focus on acing all your courses in all your exams, and you would be surprised at how fast you will end up getting to the big goal you have set for yourself.

Understand that even the best of plans is not that foolproof. One of the reasons why you never get much done is the fact that you spend a lot of time planning and analyzing how you will have the perfect thing happen for you. While it is excellent to be meticulous, it is worthy to note that even the best and most detailed plans are still not immune to suffering from a few unforeseen circumstances. This knowledge will make you know that the best thing to do is to live in the now and take the days as they show up. Things do not always happen as you would want them to, and you should have this in mind as you walk through your everyday life.

5

TAKE CONTROL OF YOUR EMOTIONS

*L*isten to Yourself; this takes us back to the importance of positive self-talk. To tame your thoughts, start by listening to yourself. Do this as though you were explaining something to other people. How would you want to tell other people about the story of your life? Without a doubt, you would want to talk about everything that you have done well. No one would want to tell others negative stories about themselves. Therefore, you should adopt a similar attitude when listening to yourself. Focus on treating yourself with the same respect that you would expect from other people. It means that you should strive to focus on thoughts that put yourself in a positive light. Your Inner Self is Listening; you should always bear in mind that your inner self is listening to your thoughts; this is the emotional you. So, if you continue thinking about negative things, your inner self will look and conform to how you expect it to behave. When thinking positively, it will also listen to you and adapt to help you perceive life with optimism. Therefore, before blaming other people for the bad things that are happening to you, remember that there is someone within you who is listening to your self-talk.

Befriend Your Emotional Guidance System. There are many cues that you can grasp from your emotions. Learning how to tame your mind can be effectively achieved by being mindful of your feelings. These emotions can quickly tell you when you are angry or feeling anxious or overwhelmed about something. Therefore, by being aware of your beliefs, you can master control over your mind before turning to think about all the negative things. The point here is that you should pause every time you notice that your emotions have changed. You should take some time to evaluate your feelings and the ensuing thoughts before they gain momentum. The effect of this is that it will help you develop an attitude of thinking twice before doing anything. Before doing anything, you will reflect on whether what you're about to do is favorable or not. You increase the likelihood of making the right decisions without allowing emotions to cloud your judgment.

Another practical tip that can make a difference in how you think is visualizing stop signs that signal to you that you should stop thinking about something. Your stop signs will warrant that you can regain your senses and avoid thinking about your past or worrying about your future. The best way of using these stop signs is to remind you that your thoughts are not helping to build you up. For instance, you can come up with a stop sign that tells you that you are overthinking about events that prevent you from being happy. It might take some time for you to master how to use these stop signs, but the outcome will be rewarding as it will enhance your self-awareness. When thinking about improving our health, we know perfectly well that this can only be done by eating right. The foods that you choose to eat have an impact on your health. In the same manner, the words that float around in your mind affect your mental health. It means that it is essential that you control the information that you feed into your mind. For example, watching horrific content on television might not be as entertaining as you think. In the long run, this will harm how you feel and the thoughts that frequent your mind.

Becoming the master of your mind also demands that you stay on top of your game. You have to keep yourself engaged in positive gear. Sure, there are instances when you might slip up and think negatively, but with the right affirmations, you will feel unstoppable. Have these affirmations in areas where you can easily see them. Pin them next to your files in your office. Before going to bed, remind yourself of your higher purpose by reading out these affirmations to yourself. They can eliminate anxiety and soothe you to sleep better. Increasing your self-awareness about your thoughts will give you the advantage of identifying unnecessary thoughts and emotions. When you do this consistently, you will find it easier to declutter your mind. The notion of taking out the trash shouldn't drive you to overthink about your past. Instead, the point here is to develop an attitude where you simply admit that some thoughts are not worth holding. Practice meditation exercises as a way of increasing your self-awareness. It is the best way of raising your antennas high enough to pick any signals of unwanted thoughts in your mind.

There is a good reason why you should strive to be happy. Most people have never realized that there are adverse effects of focusing too much on trying for positivity. Sure, we all want our lives to be full of happiness. However, we should come to terms with the fact that too much of anything is detrimental. It also applies to satisfaction. When we go about chasing happiness, we surround ourselves with all the things that can keep us entertained and full of joy. The downside of this kind of life is that it can blind us with unrealistic optimism.

Indeed, without going through pain in life, it is challenging to grow. You will not learn how to deal with the challenges of life that transform you into a healthy human being. Therefore, this should signal to you that going through anxiety and stress in the short run is not a bad thing. It is healthy. There are two forms of happiness: eudaimonic and hedonic joy. You should learn to recognize the kind of pleasure that you are chasing in your life. Hedonistic happiness is the type of fun that brings enjoyment and satisfaction. Therefore, if you are seeking hedonistic happiness in your life, it means that your main goal in life is to find pleasure. To these individuals, being happy involves merely doing things they enjoy and seek things that make them feel good.

On the other hand, eudaimonic happiness refers to the type of contentment, where satisfaction is not the primary goal in life. In this case, people pursue things of value in their lives that could lead to true happiness. The striking difference in the two forms of happiness is that eudaimonic happiness creates happiness as a by-product of the things that you focus on. Conversely, hedonic happiness only focuses on pleasure as a motivational factor. The beauty behind eudaimonic happiness is that it creates a fulfilling form of joy in the long haul. Concerning the notion of taming your thoughts, you should embrace the idea of chasing the eudaimonic kind of happiness. Don't just strive to be happy by seeking worldly pleasures. Focus more on what adds value to your life, and you will feel more satisfied in the long run.

There is nothing wrong with expressing your authentic emotions. Unfortunately, society castigates people that show their real feelings and celebrates those that bottle up emotions in a misguided effort to create a standardized culture. Human behavior is dynamic, and it cannot be regulated, but we can build a shared spectrum of what is ideal and what is not. Against this understanding, do not blame yourself as being a mess or easily irked because it is the society that is pushing for suppressing authentic feelings. However, you must find a safe way to defuse negative emotions to avoid creating fear and avoidance from people around you.

"Maintain calmness even when you have a thousand reasons not to be" Even though this quote seems to contradict the first quote, it is not. While it is vital to manifest your emotions, both positive and negative, it is essential to take time before fully expressing negative emotions. For positive emotions, it might be excusable to act impulsively, but it is still advisable to exercise restraint. Remember that within the context of emotional intelligence, it is critical to consider how others feel. Your excitement could be happening at a time when one of your colleagues has been sacked or going through a divorce. With this understanding, learning to slow down your reaction can help improve your emotional intelligence. Emotions are impulsive, and you will have to learn to anticipate certain emotions to enhance the manner that you react to them.

"Emotional health affects your self-esteem" you must learn to diagnose yourself because your emotional state affects your self-esteem levels. By identifying what troubling you is, it will enable you to read more about the trigger and how to handle it before it fully manifests. For emphasis, most individuals tend to overlook the fact that positive emotions can also adversely impact your personality. For instance, if you are highly excitable, there are chances that you are likely to overlook finer details of anything and may have difficulties planning for the long-term. In other terms, excessively manifesting positive emotions can make you highly vulnerable to environmental factors, as any significant change may make it difficult for you to recover.

Equally important is that part of your self-esteem constitutes the self-assurance that you can navigate any situation. For this reason, you must experience or become aware of both negative and positive emotions. As expected, building the ability to recognize your emotional health and attend to it happens over time with guidance and commitment. Once you master the art of diagnosing and fixing your emotional health, then your levels of self-esteem will increase, as you are likely to navigate any situation. Simply put, adverse emotional health will lower your self-esteem levels. One of the ways of diagnosing yourself is through meditation and learning to extricate yourself from your thoughts to develop an independent view of the situation.

"Life is an active process" Through acknowledging that life is an active process, you recognize that human behavior and actions are dynamic.

Human behavior is both predictable and uncertain. What differentiates an emotionally stable person from a highly sensitive individual is their emotional intelligence levels. Individuals regarded as emotionally permanent exhibit the desired ability to express both negative and positive emotions acceptably through training or experience. The emphasis is on the degree of reacting to emotions and that all emotions should be shown. Locking up emotions is counterproductive as, at one point, you will experience an emotional outburst or get overwhelmed by the feelings and make an irrational and sometimes fatal decision. You should remember that bottling up emotions could be a danger not only to you but to those around, including physical systems, if you work in critical installations.

Since life is an active process, you should accept that learning would not stop. There will be new techniques and suggestions that are new to you, and it will require mentorship and training to master them. All these realizations encourage us to try learning about emotional intelligence since life is an active process, and there are high chances of improving our emotional intelligence. From the feedback you gather about the way you react to particular situations, you should seek ways to acknowledge and manage the specific reaction. Adjusting your emotional intelligence level to desirable levels are informed by the fact the human mind and emotional state can be altered. These realizations are the core pillars of advancing emotional intelligence as a concept to be learned, internalized, and operationalized.

For example, remember when you used to cry when left alone as a child, but as you grew up, you started cherishing freedom. As a toddler, your mind and exposure had only assured you that you could only be safe around your parents or caregiver. The extrication of the caregiver from your life temporarily generated uncertainty and unfamiliarity. You expressed the negative emotions by crying continuously. However, as you grew, you learned to convert the absence of caregivers in your life temporarily as an opportunity to explore yourself and your environment. The temporary freedom granted you a chance to express positive emotions in the form of feeling energized, playful, and confident. What we learn from this simple illustration is that life is an active process, and we express certain emotions based on our understanding of our self and the immediate environment. Emotional intelligence can be learned by manipulating the internal and external factors that make us react in a specific manner.

"Through enlarging the acknowledgment spectrum, your emotional intelligence begins to grow."

Through this statement, we learned that loosening up and being open-minded up can lessen the need to bottle up emotions as well as increasing chances of manifesting negative emotions. As indicated earlier, stereotypes and other prejudices predispose you to make premature judgments that compromise empathy in interactions. Furthermore, sustaining prejudices requires significant mental while denying you numerous opportunities to recognize positive emotions. At an individual level, lack of being open-minded may use up your physical and mental energy as you try to force a conclusion where it should not suffice. Therefore, learning to allow a significant degree of freedom before concluding allows you more options, some of which are likely to lead to a decreased need to manifest negative emotions.

Additionally, being open-minded increases empathy quality in conversations. Think of trying to have a conversation with a divorcee as having performed an opinion that divorcees entered a marriage institution before adequately courting.

While having an interview with the divorcee, your mind will always extrapolate your views from the premise that divorcees come to a marriage union before sufficiently knowing each other well. In essence, you are not actively listening to the individual you are talking to because you have allowed the little knowledge you have to become the ultimate knowledge. Some educationists argue that the most overlooked aspect of learning is the ability to unlearn, which most people struggle with.

"Meditation is not necessarily emotional intelligence, but it can be a critical tool for emotional intelligence" Even though meditation has numerous benefits, it is not necessarily emotional intelligence. The importance of meditation is that it can significantly increase the self-awareness of an individual. As seen earlier, self-awareness is a critical plank of emotional intelligence. Without individual learning to understand itself and its shortcomings, there is little motivation to seek help and commit to the advice and training provided after that. In the initial stages of improving an individual's emotional intelligence, meditation is a valuable tool. Meditation can be a form of self-feedback, and it can also be used as a means for an individual to remove himself from the self to form an alternate view of everything.

However, if a person is not eased with meditation, the person should not be forced to undertake it.

"Develop healthy boundaries and enforce them" While a lot has been presented on how to be considerate of others and how to adjust your desires to attain balance with others, there is a need for setting boundaries. You can still specify and enforce limits of what you can absorb and what you can manifest. Remember that while adjusting yourself to listen and empathize with others, they also have a moral duty to understand and accept you. Sometimes not all people will easily read your limits, and for this reason, it is essential that you explicitly define the boundaries you can go and the limits that they are allowed to reach when dealing with you.

Even though it appears a manageable undertaking, most individuals set limits but lack the spine to enforce such boundaries. Allowing other peoples to overstep and violate your restrictions will reverse all gains you have made in developing emotional intelligence. While pursuing the definition of limits allowable, it is essential to be considerate and respectful of yourself and others. There is a difference between letting people know the limits eligible and imposing their restrictions on them. For this reason, effective communication is inherent in emotional intelligence.

Remember, negative emotions such as anger can be enhanced by failing to let others know of the allowable limits. Fortunately, like any other aspect of emotional intelligence, you can learn how to say no respectfully and firmly.

"Anger is not a weakness; it is an emotion, but the manner of handling it can be a weakness."

If you accept that emotions are a form of energy, then you will realize why it is essential to express them because, in this way, you will dissipate the heat and attain equilibrium. We correctly argued that locking up emotions is counterproductive as, at one point, you will experience an emotional outburst, or you will act irrationally endangering yourself, others, and the systems around you. Anger is a common negative emotion that many wrongly assume that it should be suppressed. In this book, we are arguing that violence should be expressed as an emotion. Still, it should be shown when it is building up in various ways of managing anger, such as breathing deep or counting up to one hundred before making a decision when angry.

"Sometimes spiritualism and culture can enhance or worsen emotional intelligence" There are some religious practices that infuse aspects of meditation that can help an individual attain self-awareness. By understanding yourself, your strengths, and your weaknesses, you will begin the journey of improving your emotional intelligence levels. For instance, saying a prayer may allow a person to engage in constructive soliloquy, which enables the individual to express his or her feelings instead of locking them up. On the other hand, some cultural practices may contribute to increasing emotional intelligence. For instance, Western cultures may encourage expressing of emotions while most African cultures demand that men bottle up feelings. However, it is essential to remember that cultural influence is significant to the environmental factors that may favor being expressive or reserved.

Expectedly, spiritualism and culture can also worsen the emotional intelligence levels of a person. For instance, religious practice that qualifies negative feelings as expected norms that one should live with can aggravate poor emotional reactions to challenging situations. Individuals subscribing to such methods may not see the need to seek help as such emotions are qualified as expected, and one should instead toughen up. Some cultures frown at the thought of men exhibiting emotions, especially negative emotions forcing such individuals to feel ashamed of being emotional beings. When you analyze the contribution of your spirituality and cultural influences to your emotional intelligence levels, you will pick what positively contributes to your emotional intelligence and drop others that aggravate the inappropriate handling of feelings.

"Avoid excuses as they equate to running away from reality" At one point in life, each one of us may have resorted to excuses because they provided an effective way to avoid protracted conversation that might be difficult. Unfortunately, reasons are merely a cover of underlying issues and do not offer any real solution. You must learn to face your emotions and their impact rather than justifying why you behaved in the manner that you did. Emotional intelligence offers a long-term approach to meeting your fears and joys individually and in the public sphere. Excuses work against the spirit of emotional intelligence, as they are technically lies while passionate intelligence advocates for honesty and consideration of all parties involved in an interaction.

While human behavior is dynamic and unpredictable, emotional intelligence is highly predictable. Emotional intelligence can be seen as a universal template for expressing and managing each emotional reaction. This quality of emotional intelligence makes learning and applying emotional intelligence impressive as you can develop a custom approach to your emotions that applies to nearly all of your situations. As indicated, negative feelings and positive emotions are almost finite even though how we react varies. The variation to the way each person responds to emotions varies, but the typical reactions are reasonably predictable. All these attributes make emotional intelligence highly learnable and applicable by all persons. When you start exploring emotional intelligence to improve your personality and character, remember that you do not have to learn everything in a day, month, or year. Start by analyzing your strengths and shortcomings and focus first on your weaknesses. It is advisable to learn bit by bit according to your synthesis and application. With time, you can explore the entire spectrum of emotional intelligence, including the areas that touch on your strengths. By accepting that there are several layers of emotional intelligence, you will focus on what you need and move on to the next when you have the confidence that you have gained much from the current level.

6

REALIZE THAT YOU CANNOT CONTROL EVERYTHING

There are different ways of defining a simple life. What a simple life is to you can mean a different thing to another person. However, the best way of describing a simple life is by understanding that it centers around the idea of getting rid of what you deem unessential in your life. In other words, it means spending most of your time doing what you value the most. A simple life means avoiding wasting your valuable time on things that are not important. As such, you value-creating time for people and experiences that add meaning to your life. Concerning clutter, it means freeing your mind from potential distractions that could prevent you from thinking straight and enjoying life.

Living a simple life is not as simple as it sounds. It's something that calls for patience simply because it's a journey and not a destination. The easiest way to understand how to live a simple life is by identifying the things that are important to you and eliminating everything else. To simplify your life Start by identifying what you value most in your life. Make a list of these things. While doing this, you must limit this list to 4 or 5 items. The importance of defining your list to a few words is that it creates room for essential things in your life that may arise later. As a result, attending to the first will create a more fulfilling feeling than just approaching life randomly.

It is also crucial that you evaluate how you spend your time. Monitor how you use your time from the time you wake up to the end of the day. Create a list of the things that you often prioritize and those that usually distract you. By doing this frequently, you will identify things that only consume time and that are not important to you. In other words, you can redesign your day and work productively towards achieving your daily goals.

A fundamental habit that you ought to develop as you try to simplify your life is to learn to say no.

Indeed, it is never easy to say no to your friends and colleagues at work. Unfortunately, this creates a situation where your to-do list will always be packed. What you should understand is that other people will be completing their tasks because you are helping them do what needs to be done on their to-do lists. On your end, you will have a lot of pending. It is because you chose to accept extra tasks without putting yourself first. Therefore, it's never a bad thing to say no when you are doing it for the right reasons.

With the advancement in technology, you can access information at the touch of a button. From a positive perspective, this makes it easy for us to communicate with our loved ones and our friends. Social media has changed the way people and businesses communicate. People should realize that too much media consumption can harm us. It pollutes our minds by altering the perceptions that we already have about life. We end up developing new ways of living our lives based on the opinions that we have recently emerged. Unfortunately, this is how we complicate our lives.

Simplifying your life also demands that you declutter the physical space around you. It is easy to work in a tidy area compared to a room filled with clutter. Clutter prevents you from thinking straight. Before getting rid of clutter in your mind as earlier recommended, start by decluttering the space around you. Get rid of things in your house that don't add value to you. Usually, we hold on to something without realizing that they are only taking away space for more important things. From your bedroom to your kitchen, you should work on decluttering your space. Ideally, the physical space that you create will also have a positive impact on how you think and make decisions.

Once you eliminate unimportant things in your life, you will have more time to focus on other essential items. Therefore, use this time wisely by doing what you love. Remember the list of crucial things that you created? Use this extra time to work on these things. Eventually, you will live a simple yet fulfilling life. It will be daunting to live a simple life when toxic people surround you. These are people who never seem to add value to your life in any way. The worst thing is that they drain energy from you as they always think negatively. Also, they are the people that push you around to help them without stopping to help you. Sure, some of these individuals are your best friends because there is a lot that you have been through with them. However, a keen eye on your relationship with them will reveal the fact that there is nothing you benefit from being friends with them. So, the best thing you can and should do is to eliminate them from your life. It might sound harsh. But, the reality is that you will be doing yourself a favor by opening doors for more fruitful relationships.

Living a simple life also means that you should plan what you eat. Eating is part of your daily routine. It is something that you do throughout the day as long as you feel hungry. Accordingly, planning for your meals shouldn't be neglected. Make it a priority on your to-do list. Don't waste your time every day trying to figure out what you will be having for lunch or dinner. Just plan it. The good news is that doing this increases the likelihood of eating healthy foods that contribute to a productive lifestyle. Frequently, people choose to ignore the debts that they have with the hopes that it will help them stop worrying. It doesn't help since you will only procrastinate the decision to pay your debts. Come up with a plan of how you will pay off your debts. Financially, it will help you make better decisions and open doors for business opportunities.

A simple life doesn't have to be something that is

beyond your reach. It's all about identifying the things that are of great importance to you and prioritizing them. It creates time for you to enjoy with family and friends. If everyone in the world made a list of the points and traits they think about when they think about their view of themselves, you would most likely see a lot of repeated essential factors. The mistakes, triumphs, accidents, and successes that come throughout life all carry their emotional and psychological influences with them. It's these influences that are most powerful when it comes to shaping how a person views themselves and their current lifestyle or life situation. The more positive impacts and experiences a person can collect, the better their self-esteem will be, and the more emotionally in control they will find themselves when stressful situations arise.

Confidence (particularly when described as self-confidence) refers to faith a person has in their knowledge, experience, skills, and abilities. Depending on how much belief someone has in the things they know, the things they say, and the things they do during their personal or professional interactions, the higher a person's confidence levels will be.

A person's confidence comes from their opinion

of and trust in their strengths and abilities. This trust and faith most often are the result of positive experiences such as promotions at work or awards at school. The more experience they have and proof they have been able to collect that they know or what they are talking about, then the higher their self-confidence will be, and the more that will start to affect other areas of their life positively.

Many people have a high level of self-esteem. Still, they find that they lack confidence, especially in certain situations like when asked to do something without time to prepare, but are concerned with how others will react to it. Hence, they decide just to keep their hand down.

As different as they can be, there are also plenty of situations and experiences that can be caused by interconnected levels of self-esteem and confidence. The more understanding, experienced, and control a person has over their self-esteem and confidence levels, the better off they will be in all opportunities they attempt or goals they strive for throughout their life.

Strengthening these traits not only helps with improving a person's overall mental, psychological, and emotional health, but it also comes with a variety of other benefits that can help improve someone's health and wellness in a wide range of styles. Here is a look at some of the most popular and widely reported benefits people have experienced in their quests for higher self-esteem and confidence!

Those with higher self-esteem and personal confidence are less likely to be people pleasers or develop people-pleasing habits than those with lower opinions of themselves or their abilities.

They also tend to have better performance ratings and higher success rates in leadership roles.

Not only are they more personable with customers or other audiences, but they are also more empathetic with employers or co-workers and better able to boost morale during times of high demand or increased stress levels.

They are also more likely to have higher success rates with setting and reaching personal and professional goals because they are more self-aware of their mental, psychological, emotional changes, and how it affects their daily performance.

Those with higher self-esteem and confidence levels report more personal and professional satisfaction throughout their lives. They are more likely to take up opportunities when offered.

One of the biggest problems with overthinking is

that it leads to procrastination. The whole point of the brain for causing anxiety is to push you into inactivity. It wants you to stick to a corner so that the risk can be minimized. Procrastination is one of the most common side-effects of overthinking. It keeps you in a never-ending loop of thinking that has no scope of action. Your mind can keep forming strategies and then discarding them after a point to create newer and better ones.

What you need is a plan to break the chain of thoughts and get into action. The longer you keep thinking, the harder it will get to stop overthinking about it. Procrastination can be one of the most significant negative traits of an overthinking person, and it would also support your habit of not taking action on time.

Given below are five strategies that can help you in ditching the thinking mode and taking action. You can pick any of these as per the situation and break the deadlock.

The 5 Second Rule, fear has a very deep-rooted relationship with postponing things. When you are afraid of doing something, its results, or have a distaste for it, the mind automatically starts over-thinking about it. It makes you think about the consequences if things go wrong and would also make you believe that something would go wrong. Many a time, if you don't act on time, the mind will be able to convince you that the time has passed and there is going to be no use of taking action then. The brain likes to keep you sitting tied to thoughts. That's the safest playing ground as per the account.

We only postpone things for the future that we don't like to do. People don't want to get up in the morning even though the alarm clock rings several times and gets snoozed. The reason is their dispassion for getting up. They don't feel excited about the prospects of the day. The same people would get up hours early if they have to do something about which they are passionate.

However, you can't be passionate about everything you need to do. Especially not about the things you fear or loath. Yet, inaction will only push you into overthinking.

Make it a rule to get into action within 5 seconds of having the thought. It is a concise window. But, you don't need to finish the job in 5 seconds. You simply need to initiate.

For instance, if you need to go to the office, within 5 minutes of the ringing of the alarm clock, you must be off the bed. Any longer you stay there, and your first preference would be to snooze it one last time. Once you cross the 5 seconds window, your mind would start overthinking the whole process and would surely find things to prove the futility of the entire process.

Get into action before it is too late. It is a great way to break the shackles of procrastination.

Most of the decisions taken by us are not conscious decisions. They are the decisions made on instinct. We don't put much thought into them. It happens because our mind remains on an autopilot mode most of the time.

If you have not been taxing it much about making real decisions, it likes to make decisions based on references. The things you did in similar situations earlier. Did they lead to any adverse outcome? What probability of success does it see for the actions in this attempt?

The mind doesn't like to see the probability of the success this time and the conditions that might lead it to the result. It wants to maintain inertia. It is the reason most people procrastinate and never take action. Their mind quickly disqualifies most of the possibilities without even considering them a little. The remaining time you'll have at hand now will get utilized for overthinking.

If you want to ditch this trap of overthinking, you

must ditch the autopilot. Look at the things mindfully. Take all the decisions consciously. Look at the merit of every situation, and don't try to assume things a lot. It will prepare a better ground for action, and it will also spare you from overthinking when you stop expecting a lot.

One of the biggest reasons for our backing down from taking any kind of action is our tendency to look at things pessimistically. We begin on a negative note and then expect things to end positively. It rarely works. The negative thought process is disheartening, and it is terrible for the initiative. Chiding your mind will not pump you up; it will push you into inaction.

Try to start anything new, even a day with positive intent. Don't weigh it down with expectations as that may also fill you with worries. Simply set out with a positive note that things would get better from where you start.

If you feel that positively looking at things from your perspective is not possible due to your limited view, try changing your perspective. Put yourself into the shoes of someone else you could imagine doing a better job at it. Think it through with a different perspective. Sometimes, changing the angle can bring all the change in the work.

Once a man was looking for a famous church in a village. He had come walking from far and was getting grumpy. He saw a boy paying in the way and asked him the distance of the church. I have come looking for it from so far. Sometimes we simply look at things from a tight angle. Looking at it through someone else's perspective can change the whole story. It can make the work easy and exciting. If you feel stuck at some action and feel that you do not have to go there, try thinking differently from the angle of someone else. Fears can push us into inaction. It has a powerful impact on our decision-making skills. If we don't address our concerns, it will keep cornering us. Even if we keep avoiding the fears, our mind doesn't sit silently; it makes you think all the time only about those fears and consequences of the actions.

There is no escape from this cycle. If you want to avoid it, the only practical way is to acknowledge your fears. The moment you recognize the concern, they lose the deadly impact they have. You can clearly understand the kind of impact they'll have. You also get a chance to look beyond the fears and assess the chances of success.

It is an excellent way to break the deadlock and come out of the habit of procrastination led by fear.

Our mind is continually looking for avenues to push us into inactivity. It seeks ways to push you into inaction, as that is the safest approach. Many people who began working ambitiously at one point end up in failures not because they had put in the poor effort but because their mind was able to convince them of the futility of their actions.

For instance, you aim to lose 30 pounds and get slim. Your aspirations, external motivations, and inspirations can energize you to begin work in that direction. But, it is a task that requires constant motivation as you will be working against your body. The body would make your job difficult. The mind would assist the body in it. It means that after a few days, maintaining that motivation can get very difficult. The task of 30 pounds is not something that you are going to get within a few days or weeks, and hence there is a high probability that you'll surrender.

Many people surrender even before they have begun as their mind starts overthinking about the probabilities of success and find none. Now, think if you had defined your goal more accurately and broken it down into smaller milestones. You'll lose 30 pounds in 6 months looks like a much well-defined goal. There is a target timeline so that you can't keep postponing it further. It is your first challenge to procrastinate.

However, six months is a very long period, and maintaining motivation, even with a defined goal, can be difficult. You also need milestones to help you in your pursuit. Signs help you in staging the results in smaller compartments so that you can track your progress. You need to lose 30 pounds in 6 months means that you have 24 weeks to lose 30 pounds. It brings us to 1.25 pounds per week. You will have a weekly target, and that can act as your constant motivator. You will have some weeks in which the weight loss would be slower. The milestones would push you to work harder the following week for making up for the deficit.

There will be weeks when your achievements will be higher, and the milestones will pump up to work harder for achieving the final goal faster. Quiet setting clear goals, dividing them into smaller milestones, and getting into action can help you in breaking the chains of procrastination and inactivity. Keeping a journal is a great strategy to help organize your thoughts. People tend to underestimate the power of noting down their dreams every day. Journaling enables you to rid your mind from things that you might not be aware of. It enhances your working memory and also guarantees that you can effectively manage stress. Therefore, you create space to experience new things in life. The effect of this is that you can relieve yourself from the anxiety that you might have been experiencing. The ideas or feelings or passions we wake up each day to pursue—our purpose.

7

FOCUS ON SOLUTIONS AND WHAT YOU CAN CONTROL

 e all worry from time to time. It is instinctual, as animals must worry about their hunger until they feed themselves. However, there is a certain point where worrying is unhealthy. If you find yourself continually worrying to the extent where it takes over your life, you need to take action. You must be able to enjoy your life. While you will undoubtedly worry occasionally, it should not prevent you from completing your daily tasks. When worrying becomes severe, it needs attention.

You must learn to stop worrying. There is always the chance of an adverse event occurring, but you must be able to find positivity and hope instead of dwelling on the potential for something going wrong.

You must be able to live in the moment and focus on enjoying yourself instead of worrying about what you did incorrectly in the past and what could go wrong in the future. You must be able to enjoy your life, not spend every minute of it worrying. It's essential to be able to stop the "what-ifs" and develop the ability to focus on the best possible outcome. There is a right balance between being realistic and being positive, and you must be able to find that balance. You should also become more aware of yourself and your emotions.

It sounds simple enough: just stop worrying. Although this seems easier said than done, it is possible to train your brain to worry less and be able to enjoy yourself more. However, this will take a lot of practice and patience with your progress. If you tend to worry naturally, this will be an ingrained habit that will take time to replace with better habits. You must be able to change your mind so that you may reduce the amount of worrying that you do.

There are a few ways that you can reduce the amount of time that you spend worrying. One way is to set aside time to worry simply, instead of suppressing your worries and ignoring them until they reach the point where they overwhelm you, set aside time each day to let your emotions happen simply. Instead of fighting against them, allow yourself to feel everything. You may even imagine yourself overreacting; this will enable you to see how beneficial (or not) it can be to allow your emotions to take over. Spending some time each day just letting it out will help you. You may choose to keep a journal or simply write everything down. Perhaps you type it out all of your thoughts and erase it right afterward so that you can see a clearing of your dreams right in front of you. You may choose to confide in someone you trust, allowing yourself to rant for a few minutes to get it all out. Regardless, it is healthy to let your emotions out instead of suppressing them.

Determine the root of your worries. Perhaps you have too much free time and simply need something else to occupy your mind. You may choose to take up a hobby to keep yourself busy. There may be a particular event that triggers your worries. You may feel worried while scrolling through social media, as you compare yourself to others and worry that you aren't good enough. Perhaps your fears are the result of a past trauma that you still haven't moved on. No matter the cause, it is essential to take some time to reflect on why it is that you worry and work on a solution for that.

Another aspect to consider is whether your

worries are solvable or not. If the concern has a solution, come up with a way to solve it and get it done. Instead of dwelling on it, explain it so that you may have more peace of mind. For unsolvable worries, you must be willing to accept that fact. Instead of trying to predict adverse said events or worrying about possibilities with a low likelihood, take the uncertainty. Will worrying solve it or change it? The answer is, most likely, "no." Worrying won't prevent unpleasant surprises. You must be willing to accept the fact that life continually changes. Finding the good in these changes can help you to be happier and stress less. Learning to live in the moment can help you to stop worrying. Often, suffering is a result of the past or future. We don't typically worry as much about what we are doing in the present. You must be willing to accept the past and live without regrets. Every mistake is a learning opportunity, and every issue will only make you stronger. The future is unpredictable; the best you can do is to work your hardest towards making it a future you want. However, that's pretty difficult when you spend your time worrying!

You must learn to enjoy the present, or else you will never enjoy your life. Tomorrow never comes, though. It will always be today. As a result, you must learn the importance of living today. Focus on the present. Be aware of all of the positive aspects of the present. To do this, you may have to shut off your electronic devices and take in your surroundings. Take a moment to realize how great today is and be more mindful. Accept your thoughts of the present, while allowing yourself to shut off thoughts about the past or future. Become aware of your senses. What are you seeing, hearing, smelling, feeling, and tasting? Instead of continually multitasking, take a moment to appreciate what you are doing.

The smallest details can make the most significant difference in your happiness. Appreciate everything, even the most minor aspects of life. You may live in the moment by being happier and bringing joy to others. Remember to laugh and smile. These can boost your happiness and help you to enjoy life more. Bring happiness to others, as well. Volunteering and performing small acts of kindness can go a long way. You will feel happy knowing that you made a difference and have a purpose. Be thankful for everything that you have, and be sure to help others that may need help as well. Occasionally take a moment to realize everything that you are thankful for. Find positivity every day. Take small moments to yourself. Perhaps you may choose to meditate. You may also simply breathe and focus on your breath. Focus on how your body feels and take some time to relax. You may think that you can't enjoy the present because you are too overwhelmed. Check with yourself regularly and remind yourself to live in the present. You will have to make a conscious effort to do this at first, as it is natural to visualize the future or dwell on the past. When you can live in the present, you will learn to enjoy life no matter how it is.

Self-awareness can help you. It can make it much easier for you to understand your emotions and feel more in control of your mind. You will realize why you act and think the way that you do. You can guess what your strengths and weaknesses are. It will also help you understand what motivates you. You will become more aware of your purpose and goals in life. It can even help you to understand others better and improve your communication skills. By increasing your self-awareness, you will have a healthier mind and feel much better about yourself and your emotions.

To become more self-aware, you will have to make a conscious effort to do so at first. Take some time each day to reflect on how you are feeling. Understand your current emotions, the causes of them, and the effect they have on you. You may also reflect on your day as a whole. Did you accomplish what you set out to do? If not, what held you back from doing so? Use this time to criticize yourself constructively. Do not merely criticize yourself, compare yourself to others, or think about how you failed. Instead, realize what worked for you and what did not. Doing so will benefit you, as you can learn from that and apply it to the next day. You will not be perfect at first, but if you can make improvements each day, you will be much better off. Only compare yourself to who you were yesterday. You should always be learning, improving, and changing for the better. It is a natural way to progress in life, and it's essential to do so to be the best person that you possibly can be. Remember to think about both what can be improved and what you did well, as it is essential to remind yourself of your successes and remember that you are capable of achieving.

You may ask others to help you in several ways. One way is to talk out your emotions with another that you trust. It can help you to express your thoughts verbally. You may also ask others for feedback, as they will be able to give you an opinion outside of yourself. However, this must be healthy. You should trust the other person's word and ensure that you take everything they say as a way to improve, not as an attack on the person that you are.

It's also vital that you can write down your values and goals. It will make you more aware of what you're working towards. If you don't have goals to work towards, you will lack both direction and a sense of purpose in life. Understand what is important to you and what gives you a sense of importance. If you don't have goals, you won't be able to reflect on your progress towards achieving your goals. As a result, you won't be able to be aware of how you are doing.

It's essential to stop your habit of worrying, and there are a few ways that you can work on it. You must, however, keep in mind that it will take work to stop yourself from worrying. It's also essential to discover how to live in the moment so that you can enjoy life and feel greater happiness. Stopping the "what-ifs" that you think can help you. Most of these are unnecessary, and you will feel better for not considering these thoughts. Finally, you must become more aware of yourself to worry less. It's great to learn tips and tricks that we can use to wrestle anxiety and excessive worry.

What will be the effect of thinking the way that you are thinking right now? Do these thoughts make you feel empowered to solve the problem at hand, or do they discourage you from believing in yourself and feeling capable of facing the issue at the side? Are there instances where your worries are valid? Yes! Sometimes we worry about things that are likely to happen. In this situation, what you will need to do is to face your worry and do something about it if you can.

If not, you may need to let it go. For those who are experts when it comes to worrying, this may seem impossible. However, you could say to yourself, "There is absolutely nothing that could be done to alter this right now." Then you can find some other activity for occupying your mind and distracting you from this situation that you have no control over.

Is There a True Problem to Solve? -then you might have to focus your attention on a practical solution for it. In this case, you might turn to problem-solving skills to deal head-on with the things that are worrying you.

Note: Anxiety is not your fault. Daily life and comes with stressors that can affect a person's thoughts, feelings, and everyday functioning!

Just like all other basic emotions, anger is designed to convey a specific message to us. That message could be our disapproval of something that has happened or something that someone has done. However, if our first response when angry is to vent or become raging mad, then the message gets lost in translation. For this reason, a calm mind and level-head are essential when dealing with anger. Being in a calm state of mind allows you to take a step back and objectively evaluate your passion from the point of reason. It also allows you to acknowledge your feelings and validate them without letting them control you.

Keeping calm when angry, however, is easier said than done. It takes a lot of practice, patience, and maturity to keep yourself from acting out of character when something that triggers rage in us happens. If someone offends you, it is much easier to get revenge. In a way, we derive some pleasure from causing suffering to perceived opponents when we feel like they have wronged us. In reality, however, these solutions are illusory, since they do not deal with the real issues and cause of our anger. They can be more detrimental to us and our relationships in the long run. In light of this, we must find healthier ways to control our anger, even when we feel justified in it.

So, what is anger management, and what does it entail? Mostly, anger management is the process of identifying signs that you are becoming angry or frustrated and taking the necessary steps to calm yourself down to deal with your anger more productively. Many people have the misconception that anger management is meant to keep you from feeling angry. Others even think that it is designed to help them suppress feelings. Both of these are poor understandings of the role of anger management. The purpose continually of anger management is to help you become better at identifying signs that you are becoming frustrated and equip you with the necessary skills to keep your anger under control. A lot of literature has been written about violence and how to deal with it more effectively. One can, therefore, learn the right skills for coping with frustration from reading books such as this one. However, the most common way through which people learn anger management is by attending an anger management class or therapy with a counselor.

You will get to learn how to identify the warning signs when you get frustrated, and how you can effectively calm yourself down to approach your anger from the point of strength.

While anger is a very normal reaction which may provoke feelings of aggression, using violence to deal with anger is very inappropriate. It can also lead to severe legal consequences, such as getting sued or imprisoned for abuse. If you find yourself prone to committing acts of violence when angry, you should seek professional help immediately. Through counseling and attending anger management classes, you can break this cycle of poor anger management and learn to express your frustration in healthier ways that do not involve the use of violence.

Perhaps you are not outrightly violent towards other people when angry. However, you may tend to smash or break things when angry. It is still not an appropriate response or strategy to deal with anger and frustration. This type of behavior fails to address the real cause of the rage, and only reinforces the idea that showing aggression is going to make the anger go away. The truth is that it doesn't work. The only effective way of dealing with anger is by getting to the root cause and harnessing the emotion in positive ways.

Another tell-tale sign that you need lessons in anger management is you find yourself constantly avoiding scenarios that may trigger your anger. Perhaps you don't like going to parties with your spouse because they always leave you alone to chat with other people. Or maybe, you avoid talking to one of your close friends because you feel they are too judgmental.

Whichever the case, the temptation to avoid any scenario that may trigger your anger can be too strong to resist. However, opting out of certain situations due to fear of getting frustrated is not an effective way of dealing with your anger. For one, it shifts the responsibility to the other person, thereby diminishing your power to take responsibility for your emotions. It also only covers up pent up frustration, which continues to simmer without your awareness. It can eventually erupt in very damaging ways, both to you and your relationships.

Anger management classes are to help people develop the skills to notice when they are getting angry and take the necessary steps to deal with the emotion appropriately. Usually, the classes are conducted as one-on-one sessions or group sessions with a counselor or therapist. Depending on your needs, the anger management program may take a few days, weeks, or even months in some cases. It is, therefore, essential for you to be patient and consider the whole experience as a learning process.

When you first begin attending anger management classes, the first thing you will learn is how to identify stressors and triggers of anger. By identifying the early warning signs of irritation, you can begin to understand its causes and figure out how to control it. Stressors are typically those things that cause frustration in your life and trigger pent up anger. These may include failure with a child who behaves poorly, financial problems, or co-workers who always gossip about you.

Apart from identifying the triggers, anger management classes will help teach you how to pick up on symptoms of anger. As we found out earlier, physiological signs of irritation vary between individuals. You may, therefore, not manifest the same symptoms as someone else when angry. While one person may experience an increased heart rate and sweat when angry, another person may feel a tight-knot in their stomach when upset. Anger management classes will help you identify the physical symptoms of anger as they present uniquely in your body.

Beginner's anger management is to help you recognize the signs that your anger is on the rise. Perhaps you may feel like you want to yell at the perceived object of your hatred, or you feel the need to keep quiet to avoid a heated confrontation. Being aware of the physical reactions happening in your body will allow you to take a step back and carefully evaluate your anger before proceeding with an appropriate response.

The ghost of the past is tough to go. The harder we try to push it, the more resounding it gets. It comes to haunt at the most inconvenient times. It should come as no surprise that you always remember everything terrible that has happened in your life. Your mind is a terrific storage device. It has unlimited storage ability. Scientists believe that you can record more than 2.5 petabytes of data in your brain and still have space left for more. It translates to 300 million hours of video recording space. It means that all the things that have happened in your life, positive or negative, are recorded in your mind. However, your brain also has a strong response to negative thoughts as it feels the need to keep playing them, again and again, to keep you safe from falling into the same kind of situation. It is a survival mechanism designed for good.

The problem begins when your mind starts playing the negative things obsessively and makes it impossible for you to start fresh. It makes wiping the slate clean tight. Your mind clutter has a vital role to play in this. You let your past remain heavy on you. The solace of victimhood, the desperation to stay safe, and vulnerability are some of the strong reasons.

These feelings encroach your productive space. They leave no room for positive thinking.

It all happens because you are not mindful. You have allowed your mind to remain cluttered by negative experiences and want to be in a safe sanctuary.

Let's consider a small story. Once there was a farmer. He had a big farm but had terrible luck in the past harvests. Sometimes the yields got affected by droughts, and sometimes pest attacks killed the crop. The farmer decided he had had enough of this nonsense. He wouldn't bear this nonsense again as his crops were getting ruined anyway. So, he decided to play it safe and planted nothing. Was that a solution? It was not a solution. Earlier the farmer had a fear that his harvest would get affected by rain or pests. There was a possibility that he may not get the full yield. But, his actions made it a certainty that he will not get anything at all. Playing safe is sometimes the worst move. The baggage of the past does this to you.

If you let your mind and thoughts rule your world, then you will rot in a corner without ever seeing the light of the day. It will keep telling you that the world is full of dangers and risks.

8

EMBRACE YOUR FEARS

*L*earning from the mistakes of the past and letting it go is the only way to excel in this world. If your mind is cluttered with worries, it will never be able to learn and succeed. It will lack the required potential. A cluttered mind is never able to make the distinction between a safe decision and a fearful decision.

Safe decisions are based on reality. They have their basis on the possible consequences of choices, and they invoke remedial precautions. The farmer could have made alternative irrigation arrangements. He could have employed pest control measures. Even if he hadn't done any of these, the probability of getting a harvest was 50-50. But, he took a fearful decision of doing nothing. The result was a guarantee of having nothing at all. Poor choices come from your insecurities, and they keep getting stronger. If you do not learn to fight them, they will degrade you and make you subhuman with no capability to enjoy this life.

The power to think is what makes humankind superior to other species dwelling on this earth along with us. If you look closely, they do all the things similar to us. They are born, eat, grow, reproduce, and die, just like us. There is effectively no difference between us and other species. The only thing that makes us different is our ability to think.

If you feel that most of your thoughts are negative, depressing, and self-destructive, you are not alone. It is the malice that troubles most of the human race. But, negative thinking has deep roots in the survival mechanism of humanity, and it has taken millions of years of careful evolution.

We were ill-equipped to arrange food and were practically defenseless against the beasts. Carelessness could have got us killed any minute. Our mind developed a negative thinking process in which it could play all the negative scenarios to devise a safe outcome. It is more of a protection mechanism.

If one person in the clan got killed by a beast, the scenario wouldn't merely end there. Our mind would keep playing the script so that you can formulate a strategy to avoid such an outcome again. The memory played the same scenario; it invoked fear so that we didn't make the same mistake. It helped in our survival. This mechanism of having negative thoughts has protected us for thousands of years against all the odds.

If today you are having a similar negative thought process going on in your mind, then it isn't baseless. It has its roots in the very same survival instinct that enabled you to survive even in the fiercest situations. However, there is a line beyond which anything becomes toxic. If you let your brain run loose without any control, then it will keep playing fearful scenarios to prevent you from taking action. Your mind knows that the safest bet to survive is to remain in the shell. The outside world is unpredictable, and the forces are beyond control. However, becoming the slave of this mentality is dangerous.

You are simply scared to take any action, and your mind starts showing you the worst possible consequences. Excessive negative thought patterns forming in your brain are a part of mind clutter. Your mind is filled with too much negativity, and it reflects the same in negative thinking. It can be a dangerous thing if it goes unchecked. It can make you indecisive, frightened, and weak. You will never be able to bring that winning edge in yourself. Your risk-taking abilities will end, and you will become a fearful decision taker, which means you will take no decisions at all. It is a pathetic state to be in the first place. You will lose all the control over your life. Your imagination and past scenarios will start deciding the way of your life. It will take a toll on your personal and professional life, health, family, relationships and career, and more.

Every person has negative thoughts. Only a toddler or a madman can be free from fear and negative thoughts. They are open from fear, and it has no real meaning in their experience. You, as a sane person, have the experience, and hence, your mind will play negative thoughts about things, relationships, and events. The important thing is to remain conscious of negative thoughts. If you keep ignoring the negative thoughts, they'll become more vigorous. Even a small mistake will get played repeatedly and frighten you.

If you have negative thought patterns and the fright is overpowering you and clouding your judgment, then start consciously analyzing your negative thoughts daily. Every day devote a fixed amount of time to ponder over the problematic situations at hand and the best possible way out. It will ease your negative thinking pattern, and you will be able to work constructively.

Can't Undo Spilled Milk; Make Cheese Out of It. If there is a problem, then brooding over it will not help. Think of the ways to overcome it. On a day to day basis, we come across several situations that have gone beyond our control. Crying over them will not help our cause. The only way to deal with such cases is to devise ways to nullify their effect. If you are late to work, then either choosing fast transport could help or think of a better excuse. Brooding over getting late is not going to be of any help.

The same goes for negative thinking in real life. If you are having negative thoughts, then in place of going deep into the repercussions, think about the ways you can deal with the situation. If a negative thought pattern has started and it is bringing in front of all the wrong things, start thinking of the good things you want and list the ones you can make happen. You can only kill negativity with positivity, and you will have to make do with the situations at hand. Try to make the best of it.

Negative thoughts are a torment. They lead to stress and anxiety. It is well known that stress and anxiety have a detrimental impact on your physiological as well as psychological health. They act as triggers that begin several negative processes. Your body starts releasing stress hormones that lead to fat accumulation, lethargy, and heartburn, stiffness in muscles, and the works. Your body reacts poorly to these triggers.

Trying to ignore these thoughts is going to make you even more anxious as your mind knows that you are avoiding them. You should adopt a 3-step approach to deal with such negative thoughts.

Vent: Give a vent to these thoughts. Do not be scared to think about them. Let them come out in the clear. It will help you in clearly understanding the extent of negative thoughts. Nevertheless, they do not remain immersed in them. Simply ponder over them and get over with them.

Cap: Once you have acknowledged the full scale of the negative thoughts, it will be easier for you to understand their extent. They will be less scary. It is time you can put an end to them. Devise plans to counter these negative thoughts.

Strategize: You have the scale of the problem; you have an understanding of it, now you simply need a strategy to overcome it. It is the stage where you can get help from several directions. Think of the ways to deal with the problem.

If you keep punishing yourself with negative thoughts, they will continue intensifying. Do not do that to yourself. Deal with the problem in an organized manner. Clear the clutter of your mind, and you will be able to think better.

Writing down your negative thoughts is an excellent way to clear the clutter of your mind. If you keep playing the negative thoughts in your mind, they'll keep getting stronger. The same scenarios will keep getting repeated over and over again.

Write down the negative thoughts and get them off your mind. It will help you in sorting your mind. When one thing is less to mix, your mind is better capable of thinking. Nothing helps in decluttering the mind better than jotting down your thoughts on paper.

Negativity is a strong emotion. It gets expressed visibly and engulfs your thought process. The best way to deal with negativity is to embrace positivity. There may be a dozen negative things going around in your life at a particular moment, but it doesn't mean the absence of positivity. You will need to remind yourself of the positive things happening around you.

It will help in fighting your negative emotions. You should continuously remind yourself of the blessings in life. Think about the pleasant things in life to come. The things that you love or that infuse positivity. Take a break from the negative routine. Indulge yourself with some light moments. It will take off your brain from negative thoughts. You will be able to break the negative thought patterns easily.

Most of the time, negative thoughts are very imposing. They take off our minds from everything else. They instill fear. We are so frightened that we never pay attention to that extent. However, most of the time, we are so engrossed in the fear that we overestimate its potential. If negative thought patterns are arising and fear is gripping you, evaluate its merit. Look if it can cause the amount of damage that you think.

Measure the risks and answer your fears. Do not take negative thought patterns on their face value. Think of the positive outcomes of your actions and compare if they are higher than the risks. You will have better clarity of mind. Remaining lost in negative thoughts is not going to help your cause.

We live in the age of 24/7 news channel age. Most of the time, the news is not favorable as negativity sells fast and has excellent resonance. It is intriguing, and you feel like looking for more. It is the biggest reason why most of the news items are negative. From social media platforms to the internet in general, negativity is widespread. The idea is simple; negative news has a more significant impact than positive news. It creates curiosity that will lead to more TV time, more searches, more interest, and, ultimately, more revenue. But eventually, you are at the receiving end of this negativity. It gives a bad start to your day. One negative news can shift your mind to harmful gear. You can start reflecting on all the things going wrong in your life and relate them to the report.

You live in an age where information access is instant. Do not begin your day with the news. If you must, then look only for the story that concerns you.

It is essential to replace negative thoughts with positive ones; however, it is not as easy to do as it sounds. Most people misunderstand the whole idea of negative thinking. Happiness does not depend on a few negative thoughts; slightly, it might depend on how one handles these negative thoughts.

Despite any setbacks and obstacles, it is essential to try to maintain one's sense of optimism. The benefits of avoiding negative thinking are more significant than most people think. Actually, within the field of psychology, positive psychology is slowly gaining more attention. It involves the study of the physiological and psychological effects of positive thinking, behavior, and habits.

Research suggests that positive thinkers enjoy life more than pessimists do. When it comes to physiological and psychological health, in addition to stress levels, optimistic people are way ahead of the game. Thinking positively is an excellent way to heal; however, people need to understand that they should stop listening to the falsehoods their mind is telling them.

They should also try figuring out the origin of their negative thoughts. The first thing to remember is that negative thoughts stem from wrong assumptions and beliefs. Therefore, ignoring these thoughts is not good enough. Everyone is worthy of love and happiness, and people should always remember this fact.

It is natural for human beings to face stressful situations, such as job loss, domestic conflict, and more. How people deal with stressful situations makes all the difference. According to research, however, people who have a more optimistic outlook tend to approach difficult situations more positively.

Instead of wasting energy on negative thoughts

that one cannot change our thinking about things that went wrong, people who think in a positive way take the opposite direction. They understand they cannot change certain situations and find ways of dealing with life more positively.

Thinking more positively makes one less likely to experience problems such as depression and anxiety. According to experts, optimists enjoy a better quality of life, including psychological health, than pessimists do. Contrary to popular belief, positive thinking can cure certain mental behaviors and difficulties.

People who do not consider themselves do not need to worry. Overcoming negative thought patterns and starting to experience the benefits of positive thinking is not an impossible task. Stillness, for example, is a great way to overcome negativity. People can learn to break away from their negative thoughts through meditation. Some believe that only people who think positively can engage in healthy behavior, such as regularly working out. However, this is not always the case. Although they tend to have a higher motivation to exercise, even those with frequent negative thoughts can learn to focus on their physical health by eating better and getting regular workouts.

According to another theory, optimistic people tend to have better physical health because they are better able to handle stress, or maybe because they experience less stress. Thus, the adverse effects of stress on their physical health are significantly less. It is essential to stop worrying about one's negative thoughts to enjoy the following health benefits like live longer, Prevent cardiovascular diseases, Recover faster from illnesses and injuries, gain a more reliable immune system and better overall well-being.

It is common for people to believe that negative thoughts are harmful or even toxic, which is why so many people worry about their negative feelings. According to some "experts," negative thoughts lower people's positive vibrations, keep them stuck on negativity, and so on. Mostly, they teach people to banish their negative thoughts to gain confidence and feel self-assured.

Some online articles and self-help books seem to suggest that getting rid of negative thoughts equals professional success, higher vibration, inner peace, better boyfriend/girlfriend, and much more. Consequently, people who consistently experience negative thoughts tend to wonder what to do with the thoughts running in their minds.

They wonder how to make such thoughts stop, or

whether trying to force a positive impression over a negative one can work. Unfortunately, most people tend to misunderstand the whole issue of negative thinking because they do not understand what thoughts, both positive and negative, are in the first place. The negative feelings that people have do not determine their happiness; instead, it is what they do with those thoughts.

Countless thoughts pass through the human mind every day, and most of them are negative. It would be interesting to meet and talk with a human being who never has negative thoughts. Most people carry tons of harmful trash in their minds, even those that always seem positive.

For example, someone who is walking around congratulating himself/herself for buying a new car might be trying to disguise negative thoughts and reinforce the idea that he/she was not good enough before buying the new car. Essentially, having negative thoughts is a normal part of being human; therefore, people do not need to worry about having them in the first place.

People do not have to believe in their negative thoughts. Contrary to what one's mind would like one to think, not all ideas are correct. A person's mind is just a part of him/her; therefore, it is essential to separate one's thoughts from one's sense of self. The four components of a human being are Physical body, Mind, Spiritual aspect, and Heart.

One's mind, therefore, is simply a powerful tool for one to use, and one filters one's perceptions and thoughts through one's unique belief system. Negative thoughts stem from this filter because negativity is on the screen. Therefore, when people try to heal and grow, what they are doing is changing their filters or belief system. Everyone is perfect in his/her way; therefore, people do not need to analyze and worry about their critical and nasty thoughts. They are simply thoughts, and the only way to overcome them is to stop listening to them. When one's mind is in the moment of calm, one will feel content and at peace. It is possible when one refuses to believe one's negative thoughts.

There is nothing wrong with choosing positivity; however, it is essential to remember that negative thoughts do not matter in the first place because they are often untrue. Also, they do not make one a wrong person or a lesser human being. When people try to attack and reject their negative thoughts automatically, they are unconsciously telling themselves that they are not good enough. Mostly, according to them, reasonable people should not have negative thoughts.

This belief, however, is just as harmful as their initial thoughts.

The small step of identifying the negative thought and refusing to believe it is an essential step towards growth. Fortunately, the more one does this, the easier it will be to recognize negative thoughts when they appear, which will result in fewer negative thoughts.

Therefore, thinking positively is not the only way to find healing; rather, understanding that one is feeling bad because of entertaining and believing negative thoughts is the fastest way to heal and grow. It can also help determine the origins of one's negative feelings. However, since most of them stem from untrue beliefs, it might be easier to ignore them.

Worrying is a form of negative thinking. Thoughts tend to have powerful ramifications. When people have positive thoughts and stay positive, they tend to experience positive things. On the other hand, negative things tend to happen to people who entertain and believe their negative thoughts. By worrying excessively, people reinforce their negative attitudes and beliefs.

Unfortunately, the negative thoughts people focus on and worry about having a habit of coming true. People's thoughts and worries have a profound effect on their lives. By constantly worrying about a particular thing, people unwittingly spur it into becoming a reality.

Once people understand the correlation between worrying and negative thinking, they can begin to deal with their negative thoughts and change them. Consequently, they will start to focus on things, which will lead to positive outcomes in their lives.

Pro Tip: Self-awareness is one of the skills people should try to master or at least become more familiar and practiced before turning their energies to self-esteem and confidence. Without knowing where you stand psychologically, mentally, and emotionally, it is difficult to determine where your focus should be aimed and what kinds of goals you should set to reach your ultimate hopes and aspirations.

9

MANAGE YOUR STRESS- MOVE, UNPLUG, AND SPEND TIME IN NATURE

*H*aving a bustling personality can make you feel pushed, restless, and over-powered. Fortunately, we've assembled a rundown of approaches to declutter your brain. The best spot to start to declutter your life is from within. Numerous individuals neglect the advantages allows a sound mind can offer. The mind can move towards becoming hindered with psychological weight and indeed sway an individual's capacity to work. Necessary leadership can turn into a test, and adapting to issues may feel unthinkable when you do not have a clear mental state; in this manner, it is imperative to figure out how to free your mind of excessive clutter.

At the point when you are attempting to keep

mental tabs on everything that is going on, your contemplations are probably going to get confused. Keeping in touch with them down will assist you with prioritizing what's most significant, which will make you feel less focused. You can check significant dates and updates on a schedule or in a scratch pad, and scribble down your musings on anything that is stressing you in an individual journal. It does not make a difference whether you utilize an application or simply get a pen and paper.

Work a portion of the tips recorded above into your regular day to day existence to enable you to offload mental mess. Ensure you get a touch of 'personal time' each day with the goal that you can slow down appropriately. Much the same as tidying up your room keeps it from transforming into an all-out dump, reflecting, composing, ruminating, and conversing with others consistently will help anticipate the development of messiness in your brain.

We have all heard that reflection is a decent method to clear your brain and unwind. What you might not have heard is that there are a vast number of approaches to be careful. It implies you can search for a way that suits you. Some regular things to attempt are yoga, exercise, and profound relaxation.

Some not conventional approaches to rehearse care are washing up, snuggling up, or chilling by the seashore. Do whatever works for you.

It is difficult to fix something if you do not know what's up. Know about admonition signs that your psyche is getting to be stuffed. Some typical things to watch out for are issue resting, poor fixation, and not able to unwind.

When you've perceived that your psyche needs a spring clean, the following stage is to discover what's adding to the messiness. Invest significant time to think about how you are feeling. It will assist you in identifying what's worrying you, and why. After some time, you'll improve at detecting the notice indications of a jumbled personality and have the option to halt things from the beginning pleasant and early.

Conversing with a confidant or relative, regardless of whether on the web or eye to eye, can be an extraordinary method to clear your psyche, discharge a few feelings and get whatever's irritating you out into the open. It additionally gets a new take on an issue that understands you puzzled and is worrying you. If you are genuinely battling, recollect that you do not need to handle your effects without anyone else. There are loads of different experts accessible to chat with about whatever's stressing you.

Keep in mind your past and develop from it. You can expect that on occasion you will slip once again into old examples. Ordinarily, Those examples have been preparing for a considerable length of time. Stress and blame specifically are complicated feelings. At the point when you get yourself in an old pattern, ask yourself, "How's my self-talk?" If you wind up drenched in tension, separate your stresses into two classifications: those you can control and those you cannot.

Guide yourself to Stop! Whenever stress rings a bell, or you verbalize it for all to hear, guide yourself to stop! Supplant negative considerations with positive ones. One case of a definite idea is a token of what you do have rather than what you need. It isn't just about cash yet, Also, your aptitudes, gifts, capacities, companions, family, and supporters.

In essence, making a concerted effort to clear your mind of clutter is a tremendous first step that you can take toward getting a handle on overthinking. As you begin to sort out through the fluff, you will be able to make better sense of your life and, most importantly, about the people around you. Bear in mind that if people are feeding that clutter, then it might be time to move away from them.

Schedules lighten a portion of your mental stress by making a timetable. When you have all assignments sorted out and arranged out, with spare time included between, a significant measure of strain will be lifted. You will live more proficiently and suffer from less overpowering minutes. You cannot get ready for everything, and calendars must be changed now and again. In any case, having a reliable schedule for the things you realize you should do, organized by significance, can have a considerable effect on your mental stress. Besides, this is an incredible method for promising you to have time put aside to rehearse your mind-decluttering systems.

Meditation is a famous instrument to help declutter your life and your mind. You do not need to think as it was done in the good 'old days. Attempt this increasingly modernized system: start with music you appreciate. A few people profit by uplifting tunes or great songs, while others may prefer something edgier. The class is altogether up to you, and it does not need to be unwinding music. Next, locate a place where you can disengage yourself from others and diversions.

Written words are an integral asset to declutter your life. How you utilize them is up to you. A few people prefer to write in a diary. It can be private, and nobody else needs to see it. If you are worried about others discovering your written musings, consider writing them down on a piece of paper and after that discarding it or demolishing it after you are finished.

Start to declutter your life presently, beginning with your mind. You will feel better, work all the more adequately, and suffer from fewer misfortunes. Besides, when terrible things occur, you will be better prepared to deal with them when your mind is clear of clutter!

There is a lot of power in being positive. You can make a big difference in the lives of others by being positive. You wake up in the morning on Monday and think to yourself: "I can do it! I look forward to this new day of work. It is going to be great. I took my shower and had my coffee. Now I'm ready to go."

When you see that you can contribute something positive to this world, you will be able to adjust your attitude and expectations. Think about this: our lives are too short for us to worry about things that are frivolous and empty. We should not go through our days and complain about every little thing in our lives.

Granted, many things are worth complaining about, such as a meal that takes too long to prepare at a restaurant, the gossip that's going around in your office, among other things. We can easily break down and gripe about these things. For this reason, we want to guide you through every step of cultivating a positive attitude and changing your approach to various situations in your life.

The first thing that you have to recognize is that there are a lot of challenging situations in life. Nothing worth much is going to come quickly. Sometimes, you have to rough it through the tough times to feel better about your experience. It always takes a lot of hard work and dedication to reach your goals. And often, we do not reach our goals because we are downcast from all the expectations that we put on ourselves or others put on us. In the middle of all this, we worry about getting our dreams and goals. When you have the end goal in mind, you can move forward with your life and edge one step closer to the milestone that is going to change your life. Perhaps, your goal is to set aside $3,000 for your next vacation, or you want to become healthier and work out so you can overcome depression and live a better lifestyle. Or maybe you wish to pay off a student loan, so you work hard. Sometimes, we just have to be more straightforward about our goals because only then can we have more realistic expectations of the ones that will lead us forward.

You may now be wondering how it is that you can get into a positive mindset. Well, it is a lot easier than you might think. The first thing that you should do is get a pen and paper and write down fifteen things that you are thankful for. You will see what influences your thoughts when you get a feel of the things that make you feel grateful allows.

Practicing gratitude is one of the most powerful things you can do in your life. It helps you get out of tough times when you feel stuck and unable to move forward. Also, it helps you to get out of depression when you have a situation of losing a job or some catastrophe that throws you a curveball. As a result, you might feel helpless or devastated. But when you write down the thing that you are thankful for, you will realize just how blessed you are and how joyful you can be. Life is a precious gift. When you realize how many things have been handed to you, you see that you have the support of numerous people who want to get you out of your struggles and into a more prosperous life. Think of the people who love you, including your friends, parents, siblings, and other people. Also, think about the financial situation that you have been given and the job that you go to every day. Think about these blessings and remove any kind of feeling of entitlement that you might feel toward those blessings. You should recognize that you receive a lot more than you truly deserve and that everything is a gift of grace. Instead of griping about the lack of money that you have in your bank account, take a moment to say thank you to a person who has changed your life for the better and practice gratitude. Believe that it will change your day and make it a better one.

Stop right now and get your pen and paper. Write down the things you are thankful for.

Now that you have taken that step, you can come back and realize that you are on your way to becoming a positive person. Recall a time when you met success. Perhaps you got an A in your calculus class in high school, although you did not actually like math but rather enjoyed studying it. Or in university, perhaps you landed a top-notch internship at a Fortune 500 company that eventually led to a full-time position there. Maybe you were able to get healed from a psychological disorder that you had for a long time. You had a miracle healing experience. Be thankful and recall the times that have gone by and how you managed to overcome different situations. Think about how strong you have become in overcoming all the difficulties that have come your way. Not everyone can fight the good fight the way you have. Having different psychological and physical conditions can be hard, and when you feel that you are depressed, even getting out of bed can seem like a hard thing. Once you can get over something big, you can recognize that you did it well, and you can celebrate.

Now that you have a grateful mindset, you are ready to change the world, and one of the best ways to do that is by helping others. When you help others, you can improve your feelings and mood more than anything else. For example, when you help an elderly lady put her groceries in her car and move the cart away, you have done something to help someone else. It can increase your self-esteem and make you feel good.

Helping others is also a form of therapy that helps you to make a positive impact in others' lives while improving your overall emotional well-being. When you develop a positive mindset, you can make a big difference in other people's lives. For example, you could smile and look at yourself in the mirror and say to yourself, "See, you are doing well! You are going to have a good day!" Then you will immediately feel better. It allows you to be filled with positive vibes, which help you to keep going in your mind.

The positive hero mindset can become even more powerful when you laugh. When you tell a joke and make others laugh or watch Robin Williams or some other comedian on Netflix and laugh your bottom off, you can instantly infuse a place with positivity and fight off those feelings of negativity. All of this will give you more positive attitudes and allow you to feel at your best. You should feel like you can be playful, glad, and thankful all at the same time. Being a positive hero can make you a light in the middle of the darkness that pervades this life. As we have already stated, there is a lot to be sad and depressed about in this world; however, you can make up for it by making the world a better place by adding bits of positivity, making people laugh and smile and give others a high-five from time to time. It will change your whole mindset and provide you with joy that you never thought you had in you before.

I'm not trying to paint the picture with bright colors only. It is hard to be positive sometimes. You have to suffer a lot in this life from the cares and worries of mundane everyday routine. Some days, you may lie in bed and think, "Why should I bother about all this? I do not want to go to work today." But what if I told you that it is possible to get rid of your crippling self-doubt and start living in a more positive and bright mindset every day? You can do it! I know you can.

10

BE GRATEFUL AND HAPPY

here are a few additional tips and tricks for you to be aware of to help you to make better progress towards your goals and to make it easier for you to accomplish what you want to. You may work on improving your health, as it affects everything you do. Having the proper mindset will also help you, as you can accomplish more and feel better when you have the appropriate mindset. You may also learn some additional tips and tricks regarding goal-setting and how to establish new habits.

You may learn how to improve your mental and physical health. Your health affects everything that you do. When you are physically healthy, you will have more motivation and energy so that you can accomplish more. You will feel better and feel more motivated to get out and make progress towards achieving your goals. Your physical health directly affects your mental health. If you are physically healthy, you will feel more confident. Having good physical health will also help you to recognize that you are capable of achieving your goals. When you are mentally healthy, you will be less stressed and anxious. You won't worry as much, and you will be able to focus more on what's important. You will be in a better place and be able to make decisions better. You will also improve your relationships with others and communicate more effectively. The following are some tips and tricks for improving your health.

Find out if you are the proper weight. The best way to do so is to consult a medical professional. If you are overweight or obese, you are significantly increasing your risk for a variety of health problems, and you must take action and make progress towards being your ideal weight. Being overweight can increase your risk for health conditions, as well as physical injuries and pain. When you are not physically healthy, you will not feel as well and will feel unmotivated to get out and accomplish your goals. You may also feel self-conscious and lack confidence in yourself as a result.

Practice morning and night-time routines. By having a set routine in the morning, you are starting on the right foot and setting yourself up for success. It will get you in the right headspace to be productive throughout the day. You may take a shower, eat breakfast, go for a run, go over your to-do list, or whatever it is that helps you to get motivated and ready for the day. Having a night-time routine is excellent so that you can unwind, relax, and get ready for bed. It will help you to fall asleep faster and stay asleep throughout the night. It can help you if you are stressed, anxious, or tend to overthink. You may also establish a skincare routine so that you take care of your skin correctly. Do not forget to use sunscreen every day as well so that you can protect your skin daily.

There are some other simple ways to improve your health. Going to bed at a decent time can help you to get a proper amount of sleep. Having good posture can improve your muscular fitness. Doing puzzles and reading books are great ways to stimulate your mind. Swapping out junk food for more nourishing food will fuel your body more effectively. Making simple exercise swaps such as taking the stairs instead of the elevator and parking farther will get you to exercise a bit more. Also, remember to stretch regularly (and after using) to avoid injury and increase your flexibility.

Your mindset can make or break you. If you have the proper mindset, you will view life much more positively. You will be able to bounce back quickly after hitting an obstacle or having an issue. You will see the world as a much more positive place with infinite room to grow and improve. It will also be easier for you to find motivation and push yourself to work towards your goals. You will enjoy learning and bettering yourself, and it will be easy for you to establish new habits and live a healthier life. The proper mindset can make a world of difference for you.

To improve your mindset, you can start your day with positive affirmations. Tell yourself how wonderful you are. Remind yourself of your achievements and the strengths that you have. You may also focus on what you are grateful for and everything good in your life. Remember to laugh. To cope with adverse situations, find humor, and enjoy a good laugh. The entity does not have to be so severe, after all. Remember that failures make the most significant lessons, and you can learn from your mistakes. Think highly of yourself and learn to live with no regrets. Even if you could have done something, you didn't. Everything happens for a reason, and everything that has happened in the past has led to this moment. Appreciate that and learn to focus on the present instead of the past (or worrying about the future). Surround yourself with people that have the mindset that you want.

To work on improving your mindset, you may practice breathing, which will allow you to focus more and simply relax. You may also reflect on your thoughts to check your emotions. Write down anything you are thinking: your worries, anything you need to do, what you love about life, your goals. Sometimes, it's good to have your thoughts written down. Always remember to set goals for the next day so that you have something to work towards and achieve. Switch up what you listen to. Maybe your drive to work is usually silent. In that case, you may want to try a podcast to inspire you. Listen to what makes you feel happy and motivated.

Focus on your language. Is there a way to change the way you speak to be more positive? Become mindful of this. Start reading! You can educate yourself and learn about a new topic or get sucked into a good story and lose yourself in the book. Learn what emotional outlet works for you. Instead of suppressing your emotions, practice healthily dealing with them. Reward yourself for your successes.

When you accomplish a goal, make good progress, or have another success, take time to recognize your achievement and reward yourself for your excellent work. It will keep you motivated and ready to accomplish more. You will start associating your goals with happiness and rewards. Remember to smile. Surround yourself with people that make you laugh and smile and remember to do what makes you happy.

Setting goals can be hard! You may not know where to start, what you want to accomplish, or how to set your goals appropriately. Establishing habits may also be tricky, as you must incorporate something new into your life and stick with it.

Core values are convictions and beliefs that people adopt as their guiding principles in their daily activities. They are behaviors that people choose to exercise as they pursue what is right and what humankind expects of them.

Core Values have the following characteristics: they can be specific, they can be different from culture to culture, they can bring disharmony between different people, a person can learn values early in life from family or friends, and finally values are often emotive.

Core values are of different types. Some of the

classes include family, moral, social, socio-cultural, material, spiritual, environmental, intellectual, financial, and self-care values.

Examples of core values that emanate from the classification above include respect, honesty, freedom, fearlessness, dignity, loyalty, trust, cooperation, concern for others, initiative, justice, peace, humor, generosity, adventure, friendships, and excellence.

Core values are vital because they reflect people's needs, desires, and the things they care about most in life. Core values are remarkable uniting forces for people's identities. Core values are also decision-making guidelines that help people to connect to their authentic self.

Core values are vital factors that lead to the growth and development of individuals. The benefits help people to live happier lives, doing what is most important to them.

The following are the reasons why people need to develop personal core values.

Core values help people to acquire information about their strengths and weaknesses. That is because self-awareness comes from a person being honest with himself or herself about who he or she is.

Honesty is a value that facilitates people to talk about themselves truthfully. In that way, people can appreciate both their strengths and weaknesses. Honest people do not try to make themselves appear better than they might be. The value of wisdom enables people to understand themselves better and to accept what they cannot change. It also helps people to realize that they cannot expect success if they do not know how to use their abilities.Humility is a core value that brings a person to appreciate what other people are doing. A humble person allows other people to be in the limelight and to celebrate their successes. An ordinary person will not focus on himself or herself at the expense of other people.

Core values help people to learn about themselves so that people can live meaningful lives.

Core values point to the way a person should go. Core values are about standards that define who people think they are and what they hold in high esteem. While people cannot always measure up to these standards, the ideals tell them how they should think and act.

In the professional world, employers run businesses in unethical manners. Such unethical practices include lying about the effectiveness of a product or having mission statements that do not align with the company's conduct.

A person who follows his or her values will not do things just because other people think it is OK to do so. Core values help people to check whether they are consistent with what they believe is essential.

Core values inform people's thoughts, feelings, words, and, ultimately, actions. A person's values help to explain his or her actions. A person who values honesty strives to be honest. Accordingly, a person who values transparency will always try to be transparent. When it comes to material things, a person who values his or her family dedicates his or her time to be with family members, and he or she encourages family relationships. Similarly, a person who values fitness will more likely develop daily rituals and long-term habits that promote fitness.

In the corporate world, a person may act in ways that are consistent with his or her values. Since people have different values, conflict may arise in the workplace. However, companies try to instill common core values that will guide every person's behavior. For example, when hiring, a company may not control what shapes different people's values and ethics. However, the company may try to influence its employees through training programs and codes of conduct to get the employees to behave in ways that are acceptable to the company. Core values are thereby very crucial in determining and guiding behavior.

Core values make people see how unique and special each person is. Some people value adventure, while others value safety. Also, some people may value solitude, while others may value publicity. For example, a person who values solitude may feel smothered if he or she allows his or her friend to influence them to go out for a party. The person may agree to go along, but they will not be having a great time. For the friend, people, drinks, and endless conversations may be their lifeline.

Everyone is different, and what makes one-person ecstatic may leave the other person feeling disconnected and uneasy. Consequently, a person has to know their values and live by them without fear of the unknown.

A meaningful conversation is one where the parties involved are present in the moment and not distracted by thoughts or by other people's activities. Also, a meaningful discussion includes people being open, transparent, and willing to share their honest thoughts and feelings.

When a person is not open to say what he or she thinks or feels, they are most likely not having a candid conversation. Values of transparency, honesty, openness, and genuineness help people to communicate meaningfully.

Meaningful conversations also value sensitivity. Sensitivity means that a person can sense people's needs to talk about painful experiences, and he or she is asking them about it. When a person opens up about an awkward situation, the listening party should sit quietly, listen keenly, and offer a piece of wisdom when necessary. Care for other people is a value that can go a long way in making people feel better about themselves. All it takes is one meaningful conversation about changing another person's life.

A person's core values affect every part of his or her life. Most of the time, a person's interests come from their life experiences and the people closest to him or her.

If a person values spending time with his or her spouse, but he or she has to work for extended hours, the person will experience internal conflict and stress. In such an event, the person needs to go back to his or her values to seek help.

The values will help the person to understand his or her topmost priorities in life, and in that way, he or she will determine the best decision to make for himself or herself. For a person to become the best person that he or she can be, the person has to live in agreement with his or her values. As a result, the benefits will be the foundation for the person's goals and life purpose.

Confidence becomes easy to achieve when a person is clear on his or her core values. When a person is not bright on what he or she benefits, they feel less confident to interact with other people.

Core values boost confidence in that they help a person to form ideas around what the person values. That is because people's core values shape their thoughts and opinions about issues. Every person's 'point of view' usually emanates from his or her value system. That is what brings about bias in conversations and other aspects of life.

Consequently, a person's core values help him or her have an opinion, or to stand out in a matter, or to have interesting conversations and interactions. A person who is not sure about his or her values, cannot have the courage and confidence to interact freely or to speak their mind.

Observe yourself and learn, you can begin by asking yourself the following questions: What two things were missing in my childhood?

Are there people in your life who you look up to?

You could be looking up to a family member, a friend, a grade school teacher, a university lecturer, a celebrity, a famous personality, or even the person who works at your favorite restaurant. Then ask yourself, 'why do I admire these people?' It could be that you marvel at the values they embody. For example, the person who works at your favorite restaurant is always smiling when serving others, and you can see that the person genuinely loves his or her job. Your grade school teacher ever listened to every student with sincerity, and you admired her excellent listening skills and charisma.

Identify the specific values that the people in your list exemplified. Those values can inspire you to adopt them.

Think back to the most painful moments of your life. Where were you? What made you sad? If you have experienced the pain of being excluded by others, then you may find that you value inclusivity and compassion. Although pain is an undesirable experience, it helps people to learn the things that they would not want to re-live. As a result, they develop values about what they consider significant. From pain, you may have developed values of tolerance and resilience, humility, empathy, and independence.

Think back to the most joyous moments of your Life- What were you doing? Why did that make you happy? Did other people share your happiness? Who were they? What other things contributed to your feelings of joy? As you recall those moments, find examples from your school, career, family, and personal life. You will discover that every experience is essential and valuable for the values that come with each lesson.

Make a list of your core personal values. First, write down a list of your core values. Afterward, go through the list, visualizing circumstances where each value may apply.

For example, when comparing the values of adventure and security, imagine that you have to decide to go to a different country to explore new opportunities, or continue to live where you are because it is a more familiar place. Continue working through your list until you identify values that resonate with you.

There is a secure connection between confidence, emotional control, and the conquering of psychological habits. Over the years, through all of the surveys, interviews, and studies conducted, this is the most common and repeated truth from those participating in them and those performing them: no matter what a person is trying to attempt, confidence is key!

There are lots of different life factors that can affect a person's self-esteem and confidence, with adolescence taking the most significant toll on a person's view of themselves. During puberty, humans It is in these years that men and women receive the majority of their emotional education as it has the highest inclusion of factors like the following for most people: First romantic relationships (often tumultuous with lots of highs and lows), First deep friendships that are tested by adjusting hormones, changing personalities and other life factors that may arise without warning, First significant successes and accomplishments like national awards and recognition, college scholarships and summer internships, Learning to drive and understanding the responsibility that comes with getting behind the wheel of a car and developing decision-making skills that are shaped by how adolescents handle things like peer pressure, balancing their school, work, and social lives, and making their first life-affecting decisions like if they want to further their education after their required schooling is completed.

With all of these exciting changes taking place,

how could someone's self-esteem and confidence levels be hindered or even damaged? Unfortunately, for all of the specific events men and women experience during their teenage years, there are also a lot of adverse events and factors they face (in their highest quantity and intensity than most people see throughout the rest of their lives) such as: Learning to differentiate affectionate teasing from friends and loved ones with harmful teasing and bullying that comes from those to cause harm, Physical changes to their skin, muscles and other parts of the body that may require attention from over-the-counter medical products or even prescriptions from medical professionals and Emotional modification said that is often unexpected, and out of control as skills are developed through experience and education, Lots of fear and uncertainty as everything seems to be changing around them without a sense of direction or stopping point insight.

Not everyone has come out of adolescence with more negative memories than positive ones, but for those that did and find those negative experiences or memories affecting their adult lives, never fear! The following are some tips and tricks for helping you with improving these.

To properly set goals, it's important to choose

goals that you feel passionately about. If you do not care about a goal, you are not likely to stick with it. The common proper goal is SMART. It should be specific, measurable, attainable, relevant, and time-bound. Be specific about what you want. Set a goal so that you can measure your progress. Make sure it is realistic for you to attain. Make it relevant to your interests and passions. Give yourself time to achieve that goal.

There are a few categories for goals that you may set for yourself. You may set educational purposes so that you may learn more. Psychological goals are essential for remaining emotionally stable and improving your mindset. These are all types of goals that you can set for yourself.

For getting started with new habits, you will have to make a change and make that change a part of your life. It will require you to get used to it and make it a natural part of your daily routine. To properly form habits, you should focus on only one to three patterns at once. Any more will overwhelm you, and you won't be able to dedicate yourself to them fully. Commit for at least thirty days. It is how long it will take for you to get used to your new habit or habits. Remind yourself. Perhaps a one activity that you already do should go along with your new practice. You may have to give yourself reminders for your new habit. Do not expect too much at once. You may ease into the original pattern and gradually make progress towards it. Plan for failure, and know what you will do when you face obstacles and how you won't let them get in your way. Tell others about your habit so they may hold you accountable for it. Reward yourself for making progress towards your practice. Finally, remember that you can change yourself. Accept and welcome change into your life. You cannot get better if you do not make a change.

CONCLUSION

Congratulations on reaching the final section of the book. Overthinking is not a mental disorder but leads to mental disease and psychological problems. Sometimes overthinking is a result of anxiety and depression, and sometimes stress and depression. When you start overthinking, you feel disturbed, and lots of thoughts gather in your mind ruminating repeatedly. You start making mistakes that you will not notice while doing but can physically and emotionally harm you. To prevent yourself from overthinking and overcoming your anxiety, stress, and depression, you need to follow simple habits that are described. Try to fit these habits in your daily routine, and these will help you relax your mind and make your day fresh and energetic. Thus, stop overthinking and do not evaluate yourself with other people's points of view. Just stand up for yourself and fight with your thoughts until you come out of these.

When you feel like your mind is full of thoughts, try to declutter your account using the simple habits discussed. Decluttering your mind will help you to enhance your mental wellbeing. The point is, you might get back to overthinking ruminating over and over again. It will help if you learn to relax and settle your mind to keep it from continuously circling the same ideas effectively. Meditation and mindfulness are other ways to make you comfortable in your daily life. Practicing meditation activities helps you regulate your emotions and center your attention on what you want to do, not ruminating and worrying restlessly. There will be some stuff out of your power. Learning how to understand this will go a long way to prevent overthinking.

Releasing the negative energy inside you is going to be an essential part of becoming a freer person. By infusing your life with positivity, you can live with an open mind and heart that is willing to learn from different situations. Try putting on a happy face. Smile, but do so willfully and cheerfully. Then you can experience what it is like to have fewer worries in your life. Find ways to experience the joy that never goes away. Even if you do not feel happy one day, you will always feel a sense of deep satisfaction, knowing that you are making a meaningful life for yourself on earth, and you are not going to let anything get you down.

This book has walked you through the steps you will need to stop worrying in your life. First, we started by talking about the causes of your mental clutter and what you could do to handle different life situations. We talked about doing less and worrying less, getting rid of your junk, waiting to answer messages, and forgiving the past. Also, we mentioned different ways of dealing with your negative thoughts, which could come and take over your mind at any moment. Additionally, we mentioned how you could practice mindfulness to improve your mood and boost your cognitive performance. We talked about how to determine what is important to you and how to set appropriate goals that would lead you to a happier and more fulfilled place.

As we wrap up this journey and try to defeat the demons within us, we see that there is little that truly needs to be worried. Life is short and swift. One minute we're alive, and the next minute, we are already lying in our graves. I'm sure that before we die, we will regret the times that we have spent worrying about our lives.Life is precious; therefore, we shouldn't waste our time in this world, worrying about things. Although we do not always have it all together, and we sometimes break down and cry and get it all out, that does not mean we stay there. Release the energy within you that is getting you down. Get it all out, and stop worrying. That is a vital part of your future.

Lastly, practicing positive self-talk can transform how you think. Remember, you are what you think. For that reason, if you think positively about your-self, it likely means that you are being the best version of yourself. Eliminate any negative thoughts from your mind by developing a habit of looking at life from a positive perspective. Sure, you can't prevent yourself from thinking negatively all the time. However, it's what you do to manage your negative thoughts that matters the most. Accord-ingly, stick to the recommended strategies of taming your thoughts discussed in this guide. Mold your life by thinking right. Think of a beautiful life full of hope and optimism. Practice living that life now by doing the things that you would like to do to contribute to a happy and blissful life. Arguably, this is the best way of preventing yourself from experiencing the negative effects of overthinking such as anxiety and stress.

Good luck!

REFERENCES

Ali Walker (2017) Get conscious: how to stop over-thinking and come alive. Retrieved from https://www.get-conscious-how-to-stop-overthinking-and-come-alive

Gwendoline Smith (2020) The book of Overthinking: how to stop the cycle of worry. Retrieved from https://www.how-to-stop-the-cycle-of-worry.

Emma S.J. Smith (May 24, 2020) Anxiety in Relationship: How to overcome Anxiety, Jealousy and Negative Thinking to Build a Strong and Healthy Relationship
    Retrieved from https://www.anxiety-in-Relationship.

Steven Schuster (2018) Rewire your mind: Stop overthinking. Reduce Anxiety and worrying. Control your thoughts to make better decisions. Retrieved from https://www.rewire-your-mind.

Kirsty Ginman (2008) Be your own confidence coach: Banish self-doubt and boost Self-esteem. Retrieved from https://www.be-your-own-confidence-coach.

LETTING GO OF ANXIETY

A GUIDE ON ELIMINATING STRESS AND WORRY FROM YOUR LIFE

"We ourselves feel that what we are do-
ing is just a drop in
the ocean. But the ocean would be less because of that
missing drop."

Mother Teresa

INTRODUCTION

Do you feel spikes of fear followed by a shaking pulse, dizziness, and a sense of unreality that makes you think you're sick, dying, or losing your mind? Do these feelings conflict with your usual daily activities or discourage you from carrying out your regular routines? If you are susceptible to anxiety symptoms and you are constantly concerned about the next attack, you may have agoraphobia or panic attacks. While panic disorder seems unwise and unmanageable, effective strategies, treatment like the ones in this guide will enable you to reclaim your life's control.

Does overthinking affect your action taking? Do you find yourself making pessimistic predictions regularly? Do you sometimes think about the worst possible situation you could find yourself? Will you take really hard critical feedback? Are you self-critical, huh? Does something less than flawless success feel a failure?

If some of these things resonate with you, you may have a degree of anxiety, and you're not alone. Good news: although minimizing your anxiety to zero is not feasible or beneficial (anxiety can be helpful!), you can learn how to handle symptoms successfully-such as constant rumbling, uncertainty, fear of rejection, and paralyzing perfection.

Many people suffering from anxiety problems are advised by their well-meaning families, physicians, therapists, and psychologists to "handle" their anxiety. Some are given pills in an attempt to simmer down their anxiety. Breathing techniques, mindfulness, and more are also recommended.

After all, that's not a very efficient method, and it's never been. Anxiety and panic attacks require a separate strategy, a counterproductive one. Left uncontrolled, anxiety continues to intensify as our amygdala (the source of our brain's anxiety) becomes hyperactive and more and more worried.

There seems to be a unique and efficient way of releasing anxiety, but few have ever got to hear of it.

Most people are inclined either to "handle" their anxiety or to take medication.

If you have anxiety, you're not the only one — the same as 40 million Americans, you recognize the signs can hit anywhere, anytime. If you're sick of only handling your anxiety and want a naturally derived remedy, then I want to tell you that you've taken the right decision, because you've already started reading this book.

The remedy is right here. **"Letting Go of Anxiety"** tackles symptoms when they come across cutting-edge strategies that minimize on-the-spot anxiety. The book is both a helpful guide for handling Stress and a near look at the causes of anxiety. Evidence-based approaches teach you how to manage a variety of symptoms in a variety of different cases. With Be Cool, you're still ready to go.

Living with depressive disorders, anxiety, or irrational fears can leave you feeling like you're not in touch with reality. Take on the doubts that keep you back with this anti-anxiety guide. With numerous efficient tools to evaluate and treat anxiety, this workbook features the actual and current clinical studies. You will find an array of strategies to ease your fears, end negative self-talk, and take control of your irrational thoughts, including Stress - relieving and respiration strategies, recent works on behavioral therapy for phobia, lifestyle, diet, mindfulness, dietary tips and to mention a few.

"Letting Go of Anxiety - A guide on eliminating stress and worry from your life" provides a full-person approach to dealing with and reducing anxiety. This compassionate combination of common sense and therapeutic advice will help readers unchain constant concern so that they, too, can "be nervous about nothing." This guide is filled with different approaches and methods to combat both panic attacks and phobias. The framework highlighted is founded based on cognitive behavioral therapy (CBT) and is structured by ability, with each chapter developing on the one before it. You will learn to know the importance of tracking and measuring your performance and breathing exercises and reasoning skills. The primary objective of anxiety treatment is on learning how to deal with arachnophobic conditions and the frightening anxiety symptoms of fear from an entirely more comprehensive viewpoint. Self-evaluative questions, homework practices, and interactive methods can allow you to become an active participant in your care. With your quality time with this book, you'll learn how to control your anxiety disorders, panic attacks, and prevent panic and agoraphobia conditions.

The book illustrates which strategies you may consider most suitable for diverse circumstances. You can choose the method that you wish to focus on and carry it with you and make it your quickest available anti-anxiety technique. Either you are at work, at school, at home, or even on the move, these methods are helpful to use and, with action, can dramatically improve your mood, concentration, and standard of well-being.

With my cognitive neuroscience and cognitive psychology background, I have found a way to help a large number of people overcome their self-defeating habits to be productive individuals; he shares his most effective technique in this new book. The methods provided in this book will always be used, regardless of age or background, to live a life free from anxiety or panic attacks. In this antidepressant toolbox, I have transformed effective, evidence-based resources used in therapy clinics into tricks and tips that you can use in daily situations. Whether you experience a panic disorder or are just an anxiety-prone by definition, you'll find out how anxiety works techniques to help you deal with everyday anxiety 'stuck' problems, and trust that— anxiety or not—you have all the resources you need to excel in life and work.

As a leading specialist in cognitive behavioral therapy (CBT), I have ensured that this guide is entirely realistic and also provides effective guide-like recovery measures for chronic panic symptoms, agoraphobia, obsessive-compulsive disorder (OCD), post-traumatic stress disorder (PTSD), generalized anxiety disorder (GAD), concern, and fear. You will also find new knowledge on relapse prevention following effective treatment, and updates on anti-anxiety diet, work-outs that manage anxiety, self-talk and self-soothing techniques, current neurobiology studies, and more.

This is what one client has lately said about it on Facebook: People frequently come to me and say, you know, there's something serene and exciting about you. I just giggle, appreciate them, and admit it, along with God and my Angels, my secret to peace lies within the program of Attacking Anxiety and Depression. Thank you so much for all this. Kendal R, GA

Anxiety can be likened to cancer in the sense that, if not treated with any sense of urgency, it could eat deep after an extended stay in mind and cause irredeemable damage to your mental life.

You mustn't wait to allow this mental menace to put you through unnecessary pain when you have the solution within your reach.

So please keep your eyes glued, and let's take you through the journey towards overcoming anxiety.

1

ACCEPT YOUR ANXIETY

*H*ave you ever been advised by somebody to "calm down" or "relax" in an increased condition of anxiety? Does that typically help? As a lifelong victim of anxiety, I can say that hearing something to that effect while in the pains of anxiety doesn't support me. Or maybe, it normally just exacerbates things. At that point, I wonder why we think that if we disclose to ourselves something very similar, it will work. Whenever I have attempted to "work myself out of," anxiety has, as a rule, brought about me hyperventilating in an open bathroom someplace.

When others, anyway good-natured they might be, advise us to calm down, it might trouble us because there's some judgment behind that announcement. Our way of life esteems cool, gathering certainty – we consider that an indication of solidarity. Anxiety encapsulates the total inverse. We see it as awful and pointless, an indication of shortcoming. Since anxiety is compared to a character falling flat, it is no big surprise everyone attempts to pack it down with such energy. Whatever others educate us to do regarding our anxiety, our quiet orders to ourselves are in all probability harsher. Instructing yourself to "quit being so moronic" or something comparable when you're anxious is not consoling. It is nothing unexpected then that most people would want to destroy their anxiety with drugs than defy it.

Is there any incentive for anxiety? It's difficult to envision, particularly thinking about its physical appearances: perspiring, expanded pulse, queasiness, dry mouth, etc. However, at once, those physical impacts had a significant job in our endurance: we required that expanded feeling of cautiousness when we were looking down a saber tooth tiger. That is the reason it's known as the "flight or battle reaction." Anxiety is in this manner, not a lack on our part, and it's a new developmental adaptation that doesn't have a very remarkable spot in our postmodern, cutting edge, drive-through world.

Or on the other hand, isn't that right? We may have fewer encounters with hungry predators in our day by day lives now. Yet, despite everything, we have essential minutes – they come in various structures: prospective employee meetings, first dates, significant ventures, tests, introductions, gatherings with the chief, among others. Anxiety is a courier – when you feel it, you know it's a period for activity. Attempt to tune in to its message, and afterward conclude how to react. Unquestionably there are activities for anxiety; however, a little anxiety can be revealing to you something that requires change in your life.

I don't profess to offer a panacea, yet at that point, that is the point. Possibly when we quit attempting to kill anxiety, we can start to live with it all the more without any problem. If we can accept that it is a typical response to specific circumstances in our lives, possibly it won't devour us. Perhaps we can even receive something positive in return as we face down the saber tooth tigers of our day.

This leads us to the key and primary piece of this guide. At whatever point we end up in any issue, an ideal approach to begin to discover arrangement is to discover its underlying driver to realize how best to manage it.

In a similar vein, it has been found to help conquer anxiety effectively, and we need to concede and accept anxiety itself since everybody initially experiences it.

It will be ideal for reading to know more about the best way to accept and manage anxiety as a companion.

KNOW THE NATURE OF YOUR ANXIETY PROBLEMS

Up to this point, not very numerous individuals have accepted the way that tensions, regardless of whether we like them or not, are as of now a vital piece of our lives. We experience different sorts of anxiety problems consistently; in work, in school, or just in managing others or even with our loved ones most. If you are one of the huge number of individuals everywhere throughout the globe who keeps on persevering through the sting of anxiety, read this article and be illuminated that you are not the only one in your campaign to battle such conditions. To comprehend your condition better, it would be extremely useful to initially think about the different accompanying sorts of anxiety issues that you may be confronting:

1. PANIC DISORDER

First, it is exceptionally significant that you figure out which kind of anxiety issue you have. One of the most widely recognized anxiety problems is a panic disorder wherein a victim encounters capricious anxiety assaults suffering for quite a long time or a few hours.

The assaults are ordinarily conveyed with certain signs and indications connected to certain ailments, and sometimes more terrible, even a coronary episode. The primary concern here is, individuals beset with this disorder frequently trigger their assaults because of the dread of having one. Indeed, even while dozing, the assaults can come without anyone noticing; subsequently, victims detest being disregarded because of a paranoid fear of another assault. It sets off inside 10 minutes while the victim is ignorant regarding it and may wait for an any longer time.

2. AGORAPHOBIA

Another common anxiety dilemma is this unusual panic of being disregarded in a humiliating circumstance, which is recognized by the victim's avoidance of spots that may be open. The assaults may happen alone, or some of the time may go along with panic disorder. Generally speaking, individuals who experience the ill effects of this infirmity are house-destined for certain years, which lead to destruction in their social and individual lives.

3. SOCIAL ANXIETY DISORDER

Besides, there is additionally social anxiety that causes an unwavering fear of a specific circumstance wherein the individual may feel like he is under, according to others. This is a run of the mill situation happening during open talking, or eating in broad daylight places. The victim unwittingly delivers panic on himself by only getting frightful of being in a social circle or gathering.

4. SUMMED UP ANXIETY DISORDER

Another widespread condition recognized by unbalanced tensions and worries about a specific occasion or circumstance. Clinical professionals have discovered that victims of this condition, as a general rule, experience other mental commotions, for example, chief burdensome disorder or a panic disorder.

While these four are the most far-reaching and all the more much of the time experienced anxiety problems by individuals around the world, there are endless other anxiety problems that an individual may go over at one point in his life. These incorporate Post Traumatic Stress Disorder (PTSD), Obsessive-Compulsive Disorder (OCD), or the other increasingly explicit fears setting off the anxiety assault.

KILL YOUR ANXIETY BY ACCEPTING IT?

As we experience our days, our psyches are continually thinking about various things. Our contemplations consist of the improvements around us, as we walk, drive, and interface with individuals, just as our musings about circumstances and issues in our lives. It is difficult not to think, and every day, many contemplations cross our thoughts.

Someone continually encountering pressure and sentiments of dread is truly likely to endure an anxiety disorder. Whenever disregarded, this condition may get serious and may upset ordinary exercises. An individual determined to have such a disorder likewise encounters anxiety assaults. These are critical to be dealt with because they can irritate so gravely they can cause passing. Medicine is generally accepted as a suitable treatment for anxiety, yet increasingly significant for the influenced individual is to have passionate help and discover understanding.

Anxiety originates from the way our brain has certain desires from the real world, and if these desires don't meet, we become focused and anxious. Once in a while, our inner truth isn't compatible with the external one, and our brain panics and doesn't have the foggiest idea of how to respond. The condition isn't hard to deal with, even though in the vast majority of the cases, a specialist's assistance is required. Treatment is simpler if you start it while the disorder is as yet mellow. If you don't lose whenever you feel sorry for yourself and begin accomplishing something immediately, you will recuperate quicker, and you will evade needless sufferings.

Generally, these contemplations will be general and need a superior portrayal, unbiased as far as their impact on us. Yet, there might be a few musings about issues that are worrying us, or about situations that we heighten in our psyches, ordinarily to the point that may never occur. To outline this point, I will utilize a model identifying with me with a difficulty I had.

I had been stressed over various bills that required paying, as I had gotten many in one go, and I needed to chip away at the ideal approach to meet the installments on schedule. Presently, things being what they are, I was approaching my day by day business, and during the day, the idea of the bills sprung up. For some individuals, experiencing anxiety may generally whirl around in their minds, and they may then begin to envision the 'what uncertainties' situations. This may incorporate an idea like "imagine a scenario in which I can't pay this on schedule.

While this is a consistent point of view, it isn't one that will diminish your anxiety. Much of the time, where individuals have problems is that they hook on to these musings that cause distress and make it to an ever-increasing extent, as they envision increasingly more pessimistic scenario results. It resembles a perilously crazy elusive slide. Having clarified one potential circumstance that numerous others may likewise confront, we take a gander at the ideal approaches to deal with it.

The most noticeably terrible thing you can do is overlook the issue, yet then again, letting it well up inside is no better either. Without question, the arrangement that has demonstrated to work best for me, and numerous others, is to accept the issue or thought, and therefore, even though you despite everything need to take care of business sooner or later, by accepting it, you allow your psyche to proceed onward.

At present, you may have the idea of moving around in your mind, yet you won't be battling it, which permits different contemplations to move in over it, in time. I completely value this is generally simple for me to state, and truly, it will take some practice on your part. Still, this acceptance, or taking the path of least resistance is instrumental in releasing your anxiety and not being controlled by it.

WHY ACCEPTING YOUR SOCIAL ANXIETY IS BETTER THAN FIGHTING IT

We are very much aware of what circumstances trigger our anxiety and how to commonly react to those circumstances for those of us with social anxiety. If we choose to confront our fears, rather than staying away from them and fleeing, regularly, a scope of insubordinate and irate thoughts enter our thoughts towards ourselves and our apparent failure to encounter these circumstances without any difficulty. Thoughts, for example, "Why is this happening to me? I'm tired of this. I'm not letting this happen this time; simply watch! This is ridiculous, and I have the right to have a happy life like Julie over yonder. For what reason wouldn't I be able to be all the more cordial like her? I'm so distracted at this moment, and I can't stand it. I can't stand myself. On the off chance that I can't overcome this gathering, at that point, it's done; I should simply abandon myself and go live in a cave."

Presently, how regularly has having thoughts like any of those made your social anxiety situation better? How regularly has the resistance, the anger, the self-pity, and undermining yourself made a circumstance turn out where you were totally glad for yourself a while later and had the option to handle the sentiments of social anxiety effectively? As a rule, it most likely didn't turn out decidedly. More than likely, you came out of the circumstance feeling truly crushed, troubled, tired from the inner battling. You perhaps befuddled pretty much all the emotions you're feeling in the wake of being on a psychological roll-a-napkin with precisely seven circles.

What's going on is that you are attempting to defeat one negative thought with another negative thought. You are battling against your fear with outrage, or attempting to coerce your dread with dangers of surrendering or cause your dread to disappear by insubordinately proclaiming that you don't merit this issue. Attempting to overrule one negative thought with another will never really fix your social anxiety; it will simply exacerbate it. It resembles supplanting one awful government official with another. Is it safe to say that anything was truly cultivated? No, and here and there, it exacerbates things. If you don't satisfy your psychological resistance or outrage, you'll begin to thrash yourself over, not pounding yourself! This is an endless loop that is foolish and ineffective to your progress, most definitely.

One important step in cognitive and conduct treatment is to recognize and accept the negative thoughts. To recognize your negative thinking implies that you know how programmed negative thoughts are beginning to sneak in - or kick the entryway in - relying upon how extreme the thoughts are. Rather than battling the thought and attempting to overwhelm it forcefully, try to welcome the negative thought as it's strolling through the entryway that you're so charitably holding open. You accept that you have the negative thought, and let yourself realize that you are not an awful individual for having these thoughts! For instance, rather than mentally flogging yourself to think that you can't get yourself to present yourself in front of a gathering, you can let yourself know, "Ah indeed, I'm having the thought that I'm going to wreck my name before the gathering. Much obliged to your mind for putting this thought there. I wager many individuals get apprehensive presenting themselves. It's not simply me. It's OK. I will be fine in the end."

Here's another example - Do you know somebody that continually has a similar argument repeatedly, every time a specific subject comes up? Has it become entirely unsurprising now at family parties or games with friends that you and someone, in particular, will go at it, not surprisingly, arguing your point away? What were to occur if you met that individual, the difficult subject came up of course, and you just said "I'm not going to argue with you? I invite your feeling, and it is as it is." Can you constantly imagine the stress and time you simply spared yourself from the recognizable and common argument? Wouldn't it feel great to simply not part with that energy in a negative form that leaves you feeling furious and tired a short time later? Simply think about what other fun things you can discuss with this person since the regular old tired contention isn't going on. It's a pleasant inclination! It would come as an invite alleviation! Also, that is the objective of recognizing and accepting the way that you are having negative thoughts.

Try not to misjudge what's been referenced so far... you don't simply accept the thought and leave it. You're not accepting the thought like there is no way around it. There is another progression that is vital to accepting the thought.

After recognizing and accepting the way you are having negative thoughts, the following significant step is to meet the thought with reasonable thought. Not a furious one, not a resistant one, however, a rational thought. Take some full breaths, and think about it, and glance around. In the previous model about the dread of presenting yourself in the gathering, some level headed thoughts: "I'm certain I'm by all accounts, not the only individual anxious here. What is the most terrible that can occur? This is a room of grown-ups, do I truly think they'd be immature to snap at me? I'm checking out of the room, and many people are playing on their phones. Nobody will give me an audience, and nobody is looking at me. The introduction is short. It will be over before I know it. I'll do as well as can be expected, and that is adequate. Regardless of whether I do fail, these people won't think about it after leaving here, not to mention 5 seconds after I finish. I'm truly making too big a deal out of this. How about we do this, and proceed onward."

The significant lesson is to welcome the negative thoughts with conventional thinking. If you do this regularly enough, it gets simpler and simpler, with the objective being to dispose of the programmed negative thinking and supplanting it with rational thinking. For some people, this will take some genuine devotion to practice this procedure each time the circumstance emerges. It's likewise imperative to recall that you can't pummel yourself if the method doesn't work from the outset. Continue rehearsing. Mishaps are ordinary, however, continue working through the misfortunes. Be kind to yourself, and have empathy and tolerance with yourself. Programmed negative thinking could have been strengthened inside your psyche for quite a long time; you can't hope to address it immediately.

While beating your social anxiety, work more efficiently. Furthermore, by more brilliant that implies with tranquility, acceptance, and cognitive thinking. Concerning anything worth having, you'll, despite everything, need to work with constancy and commitment to conquer social anxiety. However, you'll be doing it in a canny way. Utilizing the method of reasoning takes less vitality than any negative thinking or negative feeling there is.

5 AFFIRMING WAYS TO ACCEPT DEPRESSION AND ANXIETY SYMPTOMS

I lived much of my entire life fleeing from anxiety and depression before I eventually realized how much an overwhelming and futile waste of time. Since I accept the fact that I am an entire but imperfect human, I am safer, easier, and quieter than I have always been.

The burden of self - efficacy and work-related tension contributed to the mental health diagnosis throughout the early twenties. As a newly hired accountant with a great future in front of me, I was confident that this was only a tiny speck on my life plan. I used to take drugs, have treatment, and I got "healed" and just finished my therapy.

After five years, I did crash. My treatment plan has been extended to include anxiety symptoms. I was unable to work, drive, or even go outside alone for several months. It took a lot longer to heal this moment, however, I achieved it. As with my original depressive episode, I was determined that this was never happening again. I was healed for real the whole time!

Huge kudos to a certain short-sighted perspective, I've had a lot of depressive episodes in the coming years. I spent so much time and effort on ensuring my person was stable and optimistic despite constant nervous sensations that, when I finally see beyond the presumption, the trajectory would easily turn to anxiety and despair. I would resent myself, deride myself, and take quite a while to recover.

At the end of the day, I understood that I had to recognize my depression and anxiety for what it really is: an important part of my mindset. I can't deny that any more than I can completely ignore my left arm. Acceptance was overwhelming initially, and that was the most empowering step I've ever implemented.

HERE ARE SOME OF MY TIPS FOR WHAT ACCEPTANCE MEANS TO ME:

#1) ACCEPT THAT IT'S OK NOT TO BE OK

In such a universe that unceasingly asks us to be the ideal size of 6, get the best grades. As such, it is unavoidable that we will not be able to match up to the requirements — especially if we can have anxieties and depression to deal with.

That was such a comfort to allow myself to be deeply flawed and to make mistakes. After any depressive episode, I suspended hurting myself. I permitted myself lazy days when my thoughts were overburdened. I decided to tell myself that I was losing my mind. And anyway, haven't there been adequate fights in this universe to battle with your conscious mind?

#2) ACCEPT THAT LIFE IS A LOTTERY

Whenever things got bad, I absolutely believed that the world was out just to get me. Did you know how impossible it is? I don't think I'm so critical that the world should have been concerned about me. Terrible things happen to every one of you. Sometimes it isn't fair, sometimes it's intolerable — however, it's not subjective.

#3) ACCEPT THAT THERE IS SOMETHING GOOD IN EVERY SITUATION

On a slightly related note, I'm now trying to find something positive in every circumstance. If this is a terrible, life-changing scenario, I'm trying my hardest to see the positive. This doesn't come naturally, so I have to push myself through it, but I've never come up with a strong fat zilch, no matter how terrible my conditions were.

#4) ACCEPT THE BACKGROUND NOISE

Oh, I can't think clearly. I'm even worse at calming at a time when I really need to be relaxing, like on holiday or on vacation time. My imagination goes into hyperdrive thinking of a million worst possible scenarios. My body is on the sand, however, my mind is in chaos because I might have skipped an important deadline.

Now, instead of relying on myself for my struggle to relax, I understand that perhaps the worries are coming. I acknowledge that I don't want to get involved in every devastating scenario that comes into my head. I can concentrate my mind on having fun, even though I'm not totally free of concern.

#5) Accept who you are, but believe in who you one day might be

After the inception of my acceptance policy, I wrote a journal, married, and established my own business. Yeah, I do have symptoms, and I'm quite far more than my diagnosis.

I managed to stop condemning myself and identifying myself as "weak." I accept myself as thought the entire person with inadequacies and many abilities and a lot to be thankful for.

2

BE PRESENT, LIVE IN THE MOMENT

We often hear people speaking about the importance of living in the moment. We might learn about the various ways we 're going to profit from it. This all sounds good, but how can we survive in a moment when our minds are always spinning, thinking about the past or the future?

In this chapter, we will explore some of the advantages of living in the moment you might not be aware of. Then we're going to look at most of the challenges, and why we're going to worry. Ultimately, and most importantly, I'm going to teach you how to live right now and stop stressing by using some basic habits that you can easily integrate into your tight schedule.

The result: a happier and more fulfilling life.

WHAT IS WORRY?

Worry- Only the word itself, will start making our hearts pound and trigger fear. This is something that everyone has battled with occasionally, some more than others. It's hard not to think about, particularly when dealing with circumstances with a regular adaptation to changing circumstances. It is in our nature to want to find answers and to know what's coming. When we don't have it, our minds continue to think about it. It's hard not to do that. And as much as we would like to take the famous advice from Bobby McFerrin 's album, and, "Don't Worry, Be Happy," it just doesn't feel that easy.

Seeing as worry is something that we all seem to do naturally, it's something that we don't think about describing. We know what it is because we're going to experience it in our lives. Nevertheless, looking at the meaning of a word will give you a more in-depth interpretation of it and help you interpret it differently. The Merriam-Webster Dictionary defines worry as "to afflict with mental distress or agitation, to fuel or experience concern or anxiety."

This is what it feels like in reality. Worry is what

occurs when you're facing a significant problem; then you don't know what else to do. Your mind starts thinking about any possible scenario that could occur. You're curious what about this, or what about that. You're not taking any effort to make it different; you're just worrying about it and spinning it in your mind repeatedly.

WHY DO WE WORRY THOUGH?

Before we answer this question, it is essential to differentiate between worry and concern.

When we're concerned about anything at all, that's more probable we're dealing with a severe problem with practical solutions. And, if we do what we can to solve the problem, we're able to live with the result.

Worrying, on the other hand, requires irrational thinking. We may be worried about a significant issue that doesn't exist, or we may be concerned about all the negative stuff that might happen as a result. Then we feel unable to cope with the result. Either way, it's hard to deal with confusion, which is a normal part of life.

Some of our problems cannot have optimistic results, such as significant health conditions. Many issues are well beyond our control, such as civil unrest or debt crisis. For these cases, it can be challenging to avoid worrying, but not impossible.

Often we worry once we don't know how to tackle a problem. For instance, have you ever got a letter from the IRS informing you that you owe additional money than you figured, and you may not have the money to pay for it? That's enough to scare someone who's not acquainted with taxes.

WHY WE NEED TO STOP WORRYING

At some stage in your life, you've probably had someone suggest, "don't worry." Okay, that's helpful advice, but it doesn't help us avoid worrying. It's easy to say, but it isn't easy to do. There are indeed a lot of good reasons why we need to avoid worrying as much as we do. Worrying is bad for both our overall health.

We all have issues that affect our behavior from day to day. Actions we have experienced in the past are impacting us in the present. Things that we are doing at the moment have an impact on us in the present. And believe it or not, the things we're going to do in the future affect us in the present, even if they haven't occurred yet.

You could be wondering, "How could this be possible if such things had not yet occurred?" This is because you are already thinking about it and by so doing, that's worrisome and you're already being affected.

Worrying is harming your body. Worrying can make you suffer from muscle aches and pain in me. It can also lead to high blood pressure, reduce your sex drive, disturb your stomach, and cause immense tiredness. Your heart and lungs can also be impaired by extreme anxiety.

Worrying could overwhelm you with an extreme feeling of discomfort, cause panic attacks, and result in depression. There are all severe physical and mental health adverse effects of concern. Individuals who are suffering from depression and anxiety could have a tough time recovering from it. This can lead to isolation from relationships, social distress, reduced productivity, lack of physical treatment, and possibly suicide.

Have you ever worried about something that's been going on for so long and so hard that it started worrying you? Did you bother to the point where you couldn't sleep, got anxious, or even scared?

Have you been so fascinated with something that you can't think about something else? You may have begun to worry, get sick, or lose your desire to eat. Your output may have suffered in work or school.

If these things happen, you've made the transition to worry full-fledged. And that isn't good because it can prevent you from going on with your current life. It can result in wrong choices being made or no decisions being taken at all because you are so afraid of the outcome.

That's the primary reason why you don't worry about tomorrow. If you are so concerned with the future, you will miss significant opportunities in the present.

HOW TO STOP WORRYING: 7 SIMPLE HABITS ELIMINATE WORRY & ACHIEVE SUCCESS

More comfortable than it sounds, okay! Realizing why we need to stop worrying is perhaps not the issue, but how to stop worrying is the problem. Below are seven key tips on how we can potentially stop worrying and start achieving our goals and dreams in life. However, despite knowing how it is not enough we must also believe how it is possible to accomplish, and then actually execute and do what is suggested below:

1. STOP WORRYING THE FRUITS & START CONCENTRATING THE ROOTS

Most of us are victims of spending so much time thinking, wishing, and stressing about the outcome, and not doing any work to attain the result. The ultimate result, or 'fruit,' has several names: financial freedom or retirement, advancement or status, award or certificate, freedom of wealth or time, ability or skill, vision or aim to be accomplished, etc. Like any tree, the 'fruit' is not produced unless and until the 'roots' are nourished. Those 'roots' are hard work, everyday action, confidence and belief, conquering fear and doubt, determination and never ceasing, etc.

2. AVOID GETTING LOST IN VAGUE FEARS

When thoughts are unclear in your mind, when you have little or no clarification, it's straightforward to get lost in unrealistic worries and catastrophic event scenarios. So find clarification in a worrisome-inducing situation by questioning yourself:

Truth be told and honestly, what's the worst thing that could ever happen? When I answer that question, I proceed accordingly with spending a little time trying to find out what I can do about it if that kind of unlikely scenario occurs.

In my experience, the worst that happens is most often not as frightening as what my mind could do when it's rampaging with vague fears. Spending a few moments to gain clarification in this way will save you a lot of time, money, and frustration.

3. FOCUS ON SOLUTIONS, NOT PROBLEMS

Smart is the leader, manager, or parent who educates others to solve the problem, not just the problem. Not only is this capacity crucial for their improvement and is a wise delegation method, but it also eradicates the majority of excessive pressure and anxiety. It allows excess time and mental capacity to focus on solving the problem and do much more. Succeeding depends on having the ability to worry less and concentrate on solutions, not difficulties.

4. LIVE IN THE NOW

Wise was the one who said, "yesterday is history, tomorrow is a mystery, today is a gift that is why it is called the present." Living in the moment will do much more than worrying about the past mistakes, and the unfulfilled tomorrows will ever bring. We must avoid waiting for coming events to come and cure our present-day problems, because when these events arrive, they become the present problems, and we are still waiting for future solutions. Stop thinking about what was and what is going to be, and start enjoying now and doing amazing things by acting now.

5. DON'T TRY TO GUESS WHAT IS ON SOMEONE'S MIND

Trying to decipher someone's mind generally doesn't work that well. Instead, it can quite quickly lead to the creation of an unrealistic and even tragic scenario in your mind.

So pick the right way that is less likely to result in anxiety and confusion. Communicate and clarify what you're asking for. In doing so, you would encourage transparency in your relationship, and it is likely to be healthier because you prevent several unnecessary disputes and negativity.

6. LET YOUR WORRY OUT INTO THE LIGHT

This is one of my notable pieces since it seems to work so well. By letting your "big" worry out into the light and talking to those close to you, it's getting a lot easier to see the problem or the question of what it is.

Just venting for a few minutes can make a big difference, and after a while, you might start wondering what you were so worried about in the first place.

Perhaps the other person can just have to listen while you're thinking out loud through the situation.

On other occasions, it can be very beneficial to let another person ground you and help you get a more realistic and meaningful viewpoint on the problem at hand. When at the moment you don't have someone to talk to about the anxiety floating around in your head, let it go by writing about it.

Just taking things out of your mind and writing about yourself, either on paper or in a journal on your computer – or even your blog that's only for your eyes or anonymously – will help relieve stress and find a clear understanding.

7. DEVELOP DISCRETIONARY IGNORANCE

There are only a few things in your life that you don't need to learn, focus on, or think about. From the bombing of news to constant rumors to meaningless knowledge to conditions and circumstances outside your control, to what others think or say about you-you must learn the ability to be unaware of things that do not matter. Am I referring to current affairs, learning information, or just caring for others, and what's going on? Of course, it's not. Nonetheless, there are many things that you will choose to be unaware of things, activities, individuals, and knowledge that don't matter and are beyond your power-because your success relies on it.

8. WORK OUT

Few things work rather well and regularly as working out to relieve internal stresses and get out of a headspace that is more vulnerable to concern.

I also find that working out, particularly with free weights, helps me feel more confident and concentrated.

But although working out helps me develop a

healthier body, my main reason to keep doing it is to make a wonderful and consistent mental advantage.

HOW TO FOCUS ON THE PRESENT AND LIVE IN THE MOMENT

Often enough, we let the present wither away, causing time to race by unexplained and squander the precious seconds of our lives while we stress about the future and ponder about the by. Yeah, you 're expected to have aspirations and hopes for the future. Yeah, every day, you will take steps to bring you closer to having the life you want. Striving to achieve more and to become more motivates you and gives you the drive to keep challenging your boundaries and limitations. Still, when you live in the present moment, you do not learn to appreciate all the rewards you accomplish.

Productivity is not all about doing everything you can, and it's about taking the action you need to reach your goals by realizing your vision and creating the life you want. If that entails a lot of work or a minimal amount of work, that's a point. A highly productive person often does less work than an unproductive person because he does not spend his time doing things that do not add value to his work and life.

Buddhist have a concept called 'monkey minds,' which refers to the mind of the average person whereby they jump from one idea to another and from one activity to another Without taking the time to enjoy the fruits of their labor. What's the point of working towards achieving something if you don't enjoy the outcome? What's the point of a long journey if you don't enjoy the journey yourself? You ought to stop postponing your life and learn to live in the present moment.

THREE STEPS TO START TO LIVE IN THE MOMENT

STEP 1: OVERCOME WORRYING

In order to eliminate worries, we have to do two things:

By living in a moment, you 're relaxing your mind and being able to think more clearly. The possible explanation for some problems seem so complicated is that our mind is racing so fast that we can't see things as they really are. So we think up a lot of potential scenarios in our heads, most of which are unlikely to come true.

Besides thinking more clearly, living at the moment will allow us to think more critically. Unrealistic thinking is fuelled by confusion and uncoordinated emotions. Relaxing your mind will eliminate any confusion and soothe your emotions.

LEARN TO FOCUS ON SOLUTIONS INSTEAD OF PROBLEMS

Some people are more likely to be a little more solution-oriented, some more problem-oriented. Some of the parameters that decide this are gender, age, and jobs.

Educated people tend to be problem solvers. That's what their years of schooling are going to teach them to do. In addition, their jobs are likely to strengthen this line of thought.

STEP 2: IDENTIFY THE OBSTACLES TO LIVING AT THE MOMENT

In today's busy world, living at the moment can be a challenge. The theories are about how our mind functions, and the outside factors.

RACING MIND

A lot of busy people have a racing mind that never seems to slow down. Their minds are so agitated by too much sensory stimulation.

You see, something that activates any of our five senses (sight, sound, taste, touch, and smell) will activate a thought, and that thought will give rise to another, and from there to another, and so on.

If you have a busy life, all your movements will over-stimulate your mind and make it almost difficult to slow it down. And the restless mind wants to go to another place and time.

UNPLEASANT CIRCUMSTANCES AND A TROUBLED PAST

No one wants to be in uncomfortable situations or to remember those of the past. They can cause painful emotions that we don't want to feel.

So how are most people coping with uncomfortable feelings? By doing everything we can to avoid them, and by taking our minds to another place and time where things are more pleasant, we can avoid them.

In other words, we are avoiding living in the present moment.

Some people have recourse to doing things that trigger sensory pleasure, such as eating, drinking, or sex. Others will consume drugs that numb their minds and keep them from thinking about undesirable or stressful conditions.

A WANDERING MIND

From the moment of birth (probably sooner) to the time we die, our body and mind are active in some kind of function. It is therefore natural for our mind to have some amount of activity, whether conscious or unconscious.

Generally speaking, a wandering mind is inefficient. As mentioned above, one thought starts with an infinite series of thoughts. The reason is that one thought reminds us of something else, and this procedure could go on until we can get our mind to perform a specific function, or until we get disturbed by something else.

OUTSIDE INFLUENCE

Most of us are not fully conscious of how our climate and social expectations influence our thoughts and actions. Individuals and institutions constantly compete for our attention. Mass media aim to draw our interest to the past, and advertising to the future.

A lot of people around us who are living in the past or the future are trying to draw us to their way of thinking. Also, the entire idea of the American dream is oriented towards the future. It tells us that if we have stuff like a successful job, a family, a home, then we're going to be happy.

STEP 3: PRACTICE MINDFULNESS

So how can we live in a world that is continuously trying to attract our attention to the past and the future?

It's important to understand what mindfulness is before we get into practical steps you should take. You may have heard the word before, but you may not fully understand what it means.

Many people feel uncomfortable with the concept of mindfulness, so they feel like it's a religious activity, when in fact it's not. Mindfulness meditation is essentially an activity that involves concentrating your mind on something inside or outside of you.

Mindfulness simply closes your eyes, calms your mind, and focuses on the present moment. You 're focusing on your breathing, what your senses are experiencing, and what's going on around you right now. You blocked out the problems of the universe and the issues that weighed heavily on your mind. You can begin to put your thoughts into your mind while doing this, and purposefully choose what you're going to think about.

This is a good practice to use whenever you start to feel that you're overcome by worry. It helps to lower your heart rate, to settle your body, and to refocus your mind.

UNDERSTAND MINDFULNESS

In reality, the principle of mindfulness is very plain. So being mindful IS to be living in a moment.

If you're conscious, your focus remains on what's going on at this moment. When you are mindful, you are completely in touch with reality, because the present moment is where reality is taking place.

You know what's going on in your body, your

mind, your emotions, and the world around you. It's better from talking about this stuff. In order to develop a deeper understanding, you don't have to worry too much about them but instead observe them.

This may be counterintuitive to many people, particularly intellectuals because they are so used to logic to gain a better understanding. In mindfulness, we relax our minds and feelings so that we can see more clearly. So much of our perception can come from easy observation. As we build awareness, we practically broaden our consciousness.

In order to cultivate mindfulness, we need to train ourselves to view situations more objectively, that is, without our feelings or preconceived ideas affecting our perceptions.

You 'd be amazed to realize how often your emotions and past experiences shape your judgments. What most of us would do, including intellectuals, is make immediate judgments about a person's behavior, and then add the rationale. This is not logical, but rather misinterpretation.

If you are mindful, you should withhold judgment until you have more details. Note how I said "more information" and not "full information." It's difficult to have detailed information about something because there are limitless various factors that influence it. The best thing to do, though, is to be as objective as possible and always open to new knowledge.

Viewing the world in this way can be a difficult task, and it takes some discipline to surmount years of ingrained thought. Yet it will make our lives much more rewarding because we will be able to make much healthier decisions that can lead to true happiness and inner peace.

So if you're ready to live a better life, read on to some basic mindfulness practices that you can integrate into your busy life and help you live in a moment, – i.e., a reality.

You should not have to do all of them, but you have to pick the ones that resonate with you and fit your lifestyle.

MINDFULNESS MEDITATION

Mindfulness meditation is the central part of the development of mindfulness and living in a moment. To practice mindfulness meditation, all you have to do is sit down and breathe. When your mind wanders away, bring it back to your breath.

Notice how your lungs are expanding with each

in-breath and contract with each out-breath. Let your breathing be calm and rational.

You don't have to do it accurately. The goal is to give your mind a rest from the constant sensory input of all your activities and to allow it to settle naturally. Start with about 10 minutes a day and make your way for about 20 minutes or longer.

In conclusion, Worrying feeds anxiety and doubt. Worrying is wasting time and consuming energy. Worrying weakens ambition and leads to inaction. Worrying is going to cripple our trust, our faith, and our ability to reason. Worrying kills the capacity to analyze big and reveals an inability to manage one's thoughts. Worrying is the first step towards disappointment, reducing our ability. And yet, interestingly, it is crucial at times to stress, it can be a defense, and it can be found inside everyone. Sadly, the ability to control and train the mind as to how to avoid worrying is found in too few and yet so essential. Luckily, the learned attribute of not worrying is manageable, can be overcome, and is one of the fundamental secrets for achieving our goals, dreams, successes in life, and achieving our full potential.

To dream big, believe more, and act immediately, we need to quit worrying. Avoid thinking about issues that are beyond your control. Avoid worrying about what the others are doing and talking about you. Avoid thinking about your worries, vulnerabilities, inability, doubts, and past failures. Stop worrying about unimportant stuff, people, news, facts, and all other happenings around you which are not good enough to warrant your time and energy to care about. You need to worry less about the very things you need to worry about! --! To fulfill our full potential and achieve our goals and aspirations in life, we need to think high, think differently, be imaginative, control our thoughts and act-and the more we worry, the less we do.

3

SPEND TIME WITH FAMILY AND FRIENDS

odern lifestyle is very demanding and has many facets that need to be tackled at the same time. According to current norms, a person must remain vigilant and conscious of a variety of issues, including social status, health, appearance, a promising career, social life, etc. and so on. Attempting to do all this adequately can often be very aggravating and can lead to a person being agitated and even totally frustrated when things don't turn out well. In this whole affair, one facet of life that is likely to suffer dramatically is the time you spend with your immediate family.

Rising stresses and technological challenges, communication between immediate family members is often interrupted, and they seldom spend quality

time with each other. While some may find themselves too distracted, others may lack the energy they
need to make plans or give their immediate family
the attention they need.

However, if you knew how much time you spend
with your close family to support you and them,
surely everyone would have made it their top priority. Spending time with your close relatives not only
gives you something to do on the weekend, but it also
has a variety of health or well-being benefits.

FRIENDSHIP AND MENTAL HEALTH

Our friendships are one of the most important relationships that we have. We benefit from different
friendships in different ways. We should speak freely
to peers about issues we don't want to speak to our
families about. Our friends may be angry with us,
but they can keep us going as well.

Friendship is a vital factor in defense of our
mental well-being. We need to talk to our friends,
and we want to listen to our friends when they want
to talk to us. Our friends are going to keep us
grounded and help us get things in perspective. It is
worth making an effort to maintain our friendships
and make new friends. Friends are one of the foun-

dations of our ability to cope with the obstacles that life presents to us.

WHY IS FRIENDSHIP IMPORTANT WHEN SOMEONE IS UNWELL?

When someone has a mental health condition or a mental illness, it is vital to keep friendships going, even though people with mental health issues often appear to see their friends less than usual.

Friendship may play a significant role in helping someone to cope with or recover from a mental health problem and overcome the loneliness that sometimes comes with it. It's normal to worry about a friend being troubled, but most of us don't want to give up on a friend in pain, no matter how hard it might be to help. A lot of people who manage to keep their relationship going say that the outcome is better.

Friendships are working both ways. A mental health issue doesn't mean you're never able to love or laugh at anyone else.

THE NEGATIVE FACTORS OF NOT SPENDING ENOUGH QUALITY TIME

We all want to spend more time with family and friends, but it doesn't always happen that way, unfortunately. Here are some of the disadvantages of not spending enough quality time and a busy, pressure-packed lifestyle:

Children can experience mental stress due to lack of parental involvement. Failing academics and cognitive issues may arise.

You 're going to take more time and stay late is going to become more natural. Your friends can gradually attempt to communicate with you due to overwork.

SPENDING TIME WITH LOVED ONES HELPS

If a tragedy occurs or you have a personal problem of some kind, it helps to spend time with your loved ones. Loved as a child, a sister or a brother, or even a beloved best friend, the pain still seems to be calming and relaxing.

It also seems like when a loved one wraps his arms around a person in pain, it's easier for that person to let out all emotions. You were definitely in this place yourself.

It's much better for a person who's going through a crisis to let their emotions go. Yet if they hold frustration, resentment, and distress or fear inside, there might be other kinds of emotional problems or anomalies.

If you are in some sort of crisis or disaster, you can call a loved one, a near relative, or the best friend you really like and are near to. You 're going to need these workers to help you through whatever the condition is.

Not only can they give you some advice, because they can think and see clearly, but they can comfort and help you in this difficult time of your life. You can't be on your own or think clearly while you're distracted.

A close relative or a loved one will also help you relax because they will be there to answer a call and help with the organization of the household. This can also be of benefit if someone else is involved because they serve as an intermediary or a middle person who is unbiased.

Spending time with family and friends helps, even though we don't completely understand why, the fact is that this has been the way for many centuries and will be the way for many more coming years.

And, if you're in distress, your family and friends are going to encourage you to call them.

They wouldn't want you to go through a difficult time without them, and they might be upset if you don't call.

WHY SPENDING TIME WITH FRIENDS IS ONE OF THE BEST THINGS YOU CAN DO FOR YOUR HEALTH

Every time someone sets out to improve their health, they generally take a familiar path: starting a balanced diet, taking a new exercise regime, getting better sleep, drinking more water. Each of these behaviors is important, of course, but they all focus on physical health — and a meaningful body of work implies that social life is just as crucial, if not more so, to general health-being.

One research conducted in 2019 in the journal PLOS ONE, for example, found that the vitality of a people's current circle — as measured by inbound and outbound call activity — was a better predictor of self-reported stress, satisfaction, and well-being than fitness tracker data on physical activity, heart rate, and sleep. The result shows that the "quantified self" represented by endless amounts of medical data does not tell the whole story, says research co-author Nitesh Chawla, Professor of Informatics and Engineering at the University of Notre Dame.

Chawla believes that there is also a competent self, who is who I am, what my desires are, my social network, and all those aspects that are not supported in any of these dimensions. My lifestyle, my enjoyment, my social network — all these are significant indicators of my well-being.

A lot of previous studies support Chawla's hypothesis. Research has shown that social assistance — whether it comes from strangers, family members, or spouses — is strongly linked to better physical and better well-being. Secure social life, these studies indicate, can lower stress levels; increase mood; promote positive health patterns and prevent negative ones; improve cardiovascular health; increase disease recovery rates; and support virtually all of them. Studies have also shown that a social dimension will boost the benefits of already-healthy activities such as exercise.

Loneliness, however, is related to high levels of severe illnesses and mental health problems, and can even help drive cell-level changes that encourage inflammatory response and impair immunity. The adverse health effects of isolation have been linked to smoking 15 cigarettes a day. This is a significant issue, especially as loneliness is emerging as a public health crisis in the US. According to the latest surveys, almost half of Americans, including significant numbers of the country's youth and oldest adults, are depressed.

The research commissioned by the health insurer Cigna and published in the American Journal of Health Promotion in 2019 determined what caused such high levels of loneliness. Unsurprisingly, it has been found that social media, when used in such a way that it infringes on face-to-face quality time, is linked to more excellent isolation. In contrast, positive in-person interactions, high levels of social support, and involvement in relationships have been associated with less loneliness.

Sexuality and revenue did not show a significant impact. Still, depression seems to decline with age, possibly due to the experience and age of years of life, says Dr. Stuart Lustig, one of the study's authors, and Cigna 's National Behavioral Health Officer.

Lustig cites a study underlines the importance of carving time for family and friends, especially because isolation was inversely linked to self-reported health and well-being.

Reviving a dormant social life can be best and most easily achieved by seeking partners for enjoyable activities such as exercise, volunteering, or sharing a meal, he says.

According to Lustig, actual, face-to-face interaction with people is vital, and the aspect of the process makes it fun and pleasant and gives people a reason to get together,"

Lustig points out that social media should be used judiciously and strategically, not as a substitute for in-person relations. Alternatively, he suggests, we should use technology to find meaningful links and people that you can hold in your social sphere. It's easy enough to join groups like Meetups or to find places where you can find people doing what you want to do. "This advice is particularly useful for young people", he says, for whom heavy use of social media is healthy.

Lustig did point out that only minor societal shifts can have a significant impact. Having regular post-meeting chats with co-workers, or even multi-interactions with random people will make your social life more rewarding. He also believes that there is a way to develop these kinds of quick

connections to talk and more meaningful friendships over time. Furthermore, people have to take
those opportunities everywhere they can, because
most of us, innately, is designed from birth to
connect"—and because that will impact your well-
being.

3 WAYS SPENDING TIME WITH YOUR FAMILY POSITIVELY AFFECTS HEALTH

YOU WILL RELIEVE STRESS

There is no place like home, no friend better than
your own family. Enjoying time with your immediate
relatives gives you an overall stress buffer and helps
you reduce anxiety by having a motivating, heart-
connected conversation. If a person feels close to his
or her close family, he or she recognizes that they
have a good support system and that this can significantly reduce their risk of stress-related illnesses.

For example, spending time with your parents
reduces the stress hormone and also injects oxytocin
into your brain, which is a substance that makes you
feel good. So either you're spending time with your
children for their good, or you're spending time with

your own parents to give you up, it's a win-win situation.

YOU ARE LIKELY TO LIVE LONGER

Creating healthy relationships with your family members is linked to survival, as shown by a recent survey by Brigham Young University and the University of North Carolina at Chapel Hill. So, if you take time out every day, or at least every week, to spend time with your immediate family, it's likely to make your life easier and eventually give you a longer and happier life.

YOU ARE LESS LIKELY TO HAVE MENTAL HEALTH ISSUES

Maintaining a family is a blessing as a parent is also an established part of enjoying a more gratifying, enjoyable, and hopefully, longer life without serious health issues. Consequently, those who love their families and make it a point to spend more time with them would definitely add to their years.

Mental health is a very important aspect of a healthy life, and as life becomes more stressful, more people are likely to experience a range of mental health issues, including dementia, ADHD, depression, anxiety, and others. However, spending time with your immediate family helps you create a bond that gives you the power you need to cope with daily pressure and keep your brain healthy. Swedish study studying people aged 75 and over has shown that those who have a stable and supportive relationship with their families are less likely to suffer from dementia.

Being with your family helps you control pressure, socialize with people who can help, and remind you that you also have effective support systems that help you in issues important to you. Spending time with your immediate family is more important than going to a psychiatrist as daily family time provides the same stress-relieving therapy you pay for. According to a survey of 309,000 people, good relationships have been identified as a cause of longevity and a 50% chance of premature death. Other work has shown that caring behavior is beneficial for both the donor and the recipient and that it stimulates stress-enhancing hormones, decreasing the risk of brain disease.

YOU ARE LIKELY TO HAVE A SHARPER MEMORY

Usually, we remember things that are most important to us, don't we? If our brains are filled with valuable information that also has an emotional meaning for us, this leads to a sharper and more precise memory. As mentioned above, people over 75 years of age who had good relationships with family members and friends were less likely to be infected with dementia. Studies have shown that intense emotional experiences are more likely to be remembered and that positive feelings are remembered rather than negative ones. So making happy memories of your family is certainly a bonus to your memory, because it contributes to brain exercises that improve your accuracy in detail and make it possible for you to do more.

These results are usually apparent and markers of improved cognitive capacity and memory can be easily measured. Your sharper memory will have a very beneficial impact on your work, your sociability, and other facets of life.

Therefore, spending time with family does not only benefit them but is also very advantageous to you. As a number of clinical studies have shown, caring action is beneficial to both the giver and the receiver, and does wonder about your stress and anxiety, dramatically reducing them, and leading you to a safer and better lifestyle.

There are also other advantages to spending time with your immediate family, including your emotional well-being, the way your children are born, and the advantages that will help you improve your career. Evidence suggests that people with healthy family life are likely to gain more than those who do not have a very comfortable or satisfying relationship with their direct family. Similarly, evidence also suggests that children born in a family-friendly atmosphere are better able to make decisions in adult years.

With this in mind, let's take a look at a variety of ways that you can invest more time with friends and family and efficiently relieve stress.

1. PLAN QUALITY TIME WITH FAMILY

It may sound like an easy solution, but actually planning something is key to maintaining a healthy relationship with your family. Taking as much of your family as you can, even if this time is after work, on a weekend, or just for lunch breaks, if appropriate.

For example, planning family vacations will motivate you to take part in the physical activity that you might be avoiding behind your desk. As a matter of fact, it has shown that even spending time with a loved one reduces overall stress, so start scheduling some quality time with those who are closest to you.

2. TALK ABOUT YOUR DAY WITH PEOPLE WHO CARE

There is a reason people are thought to be caring. Your loved ones are there for you, and if you're under a lot of stress, they will understand and want to help you.

Nevertheless, a new study from Canada recently found that sharing emotional pressures with loved ones is a sure way to alleviate the stress of daily life.

Another research study showed that people get further away from those they know and have no one to know, they work far less efficiently.

3. WHEN THE WORKDAY IS OVER, IT'S OVER

Is there an increasing trend in modern labor to take spare time and turn it into working hours? Have you found yourself staying up late at night because you wanted to respond to an important email?

You bring your stress home when this happens, and it's not helpful in your home life. Start working when it's time to go home. The emails will be there in the morning when you sign in to your machine so the world won't stop between 2 a.m. to 9 a.m.

4. PLAN MORE VACATIONS

There's no question about any of it, American vacations are even less than their western counterparts. Vacation is the best opportunity to spend so much time with the people we're closest to.

In addition, taking a holiday will substantially alleviate stress on its own, but spending time with your loved ones creates indelible memories, which can be a huge stress reducer. On top of that, vacationing usually results in higher activity rates as you go out on excursions with your loved ones, so heightened activity is the perfect way to relieve stress.

5. TAKE EVERY OPPORTUNITY TO HANG OUT WITH NON-WORK FRIENDS

Spending time with your non-work mates is the secret to maintaining a healthy relationship and stress; in fact, this study shows that helping mates is critical to braving a stress roller coaster.

The study found that people who are under stressful circumstances are producing less cortisol, a stress hormone, than those who do it on their own. While you can have nice friends at work, not much contact can lead you back to this part of your life that can increase your stress levels.

CONCLUDING

Don't let your job and your responsibilities consume your life! Family and friends are there to serve as a supportive buffer for the daunting aspects of your everyday life, so use them to help relieve some of the strain. Spending time with family and friends is always beneficial and will help you fully relax after the busiest days, so don't forget to put your time in; you'll find that friends and family can be the solution to your stress.

4

REDUCE ANXIETY AND DEPRESSION
BY EXERCISING

*E*xercise is commonly recognized in the mental health industry as a natural alternative to anxiety. There is a clear correlation between mental and physical health, and improving one aspect of health can affect another. Even your emotional condition can have a dramatic effect on your physical looks.

Even changing your physical state will make you feel better. Pick your head up and put a smile to see if it makes you feel special. Exercise transforms your physical condition dramatically and can help you get rid of negative thoughts and desires.

Individuals with stress and anxiety may have little motivation and feel unmotivated to do something about it. It will make it challenging to undertake the exercise routine, but those that do, reap the benefits of the workout. Exercise lets the bodywork off excessive adrenaline. This substance is transported around the body when a fight or flight or only a stress reaction is caused.

Unfortunately, stress responses may also be caused, and people with anxiety are hypertensive to stress and anxiety. As excess adrenaline builds up in the body, it can cause symptoms such as sweating, pounding hearts, severe headaches. By removing these compounds from the body, a person can feel much better.

What's more, endorphins are formed in the pituitary gland amid exercise, producing good feelings. Those are the same chemicals that are created when you think of a happy thought or laugh. It could be a perfect stress reliever and put you in a reasonable frame of mind.

Aerobic activity is usually the best, experts to say. Running, cycling and swimming are fine, but you should try a lot of different types of exercise. The key thing is to get the heart rate up and keep the lungs working. Exercise helps you stretch and relax stressed muscles and encourage deep breathing.

Eventually, it will improve your strength and endurance and strengthen your immune system. If you are overweight, it's a sure-fire way to lose weight when eaten in moderation. This can boost your physical image and self-confidence.

Having briefly addressed the benefits of exercise in reducing anxiety, now let us quickly see how inactivity boosts and induces anxiety.

In reality, the relationship begins at inactivity. Research has shown a very close association between lack of exercise and the development of mental illnesses. This relationship is not entirely clear, but many of the potential causes of this entail:

Unused energy - among the most widely cited sources of anxiety is unused energy. The body has been made to move, and sadly, when it doesn't move, it causes discomfort. In reality, we see that also with dogs who don't get their regular walks sometimes get nervous and strung up, and if they don't work out their stress, the stress first transforms into physical tension, and then into mental tension.

Chronic stress hormone - Once you experience pain, the body releases a hormone called cortisol. There is proof that movement is what lowers cortisol, taking it back to normal levels. This makes sense, as anxiety itself is a form of "fight or flight." Once your body feels this, it wants you to fight or escape. Mostly, inactivity doesn't do anything, so that may cause the body to begin to confuse the stress and anxiety hormones.

Immune System Malfunction- Exercise is also required for the controlled immune response to keep a healthy hormone level. There is reason to believe that inactivity inhibits such critical issues from happening. There may be secondary components as well. Those that are often inactive are also often enjoying fewer experiences, and positive experiences are good for anxiety. Those that aren't working to improve their health may develop small problems that create anxiety on their own. These may all be contributing factors.

So whether wasted energy causes anxiety through a mind/body relation, or any other mechanism causes anxiety, there is confirmation that inactivity is one of the critical issues that contribute to anxiety.

Anxiety and depression disorders can rob feelings of power and meaning in life, but exercise can help you regain control of your life.

That's why we're going to focus this chapter of this book on the use of exercise to overcome anxiety.

Based on various ways in which people seek to resolve anxiety that all sorts of drugs are part of, there are still a few people who struggle to believe that discovering the idea of exercise would not help to alleviate anxiety and any other mental illness.

Now let's clear up your doubts if you belong to this category of people.

CAN EXERCISE HELP TREAT ANXIETY?

Chances are better that you, or somebody you know, are dealing with anxieties. About one five Americans aged 18 and one in three teenagers aged 13 to 18 also had a chronic anxiety disorder in the past year. So when I speak to college students, they 're not at all shocked that 63% of students experienced a lot of anxiety during their first year, according to a study by the National College Health Association.

So soon as some people know that they're struggling with depression, a lot of people are seeking medication right away. You can go to your doctor to talk about drugs. You may start looking for a therapist. You might try to take a more rational approach and use herbal remedies.

However, what you do not know is there is a form of anxiety treatment that is just as effective as other medications. It's an approach that isn't just free of side effects-it could also make you healthier. There is a system that you can easily incorporate into your life right now, and the only thing you may need to purchase is new shoes.

Something many people often don't know is that regular exercise alone can be strong enough to reduce your anxiety dramatically. Research has shown time and time again that there is an extremely close connection between anxiety and exercise-one that may tip the scales for an anxiety-free life.

The cost of anxiety can be intense: it raises a person at risk of other mental conditions, such as depression, and can lead to diabetes and cardiovascular problems. A startling study reveals that people with anxiety appear to be more sedentary and do less vigorous physical exercise if any. Interestingly, lacing up your shoes and getting out and about might be the only possible non-medical option we have to avoid and overcome anxiety.

As a psychologist who examines the impact of exercise on the brain, I have not only seen research, but I have seen firsthand how regular exercise affects my patients. Research shows that aerobic exercise is particularly helpful. A short bike ride, a ballet class, or even a fast walk can be a powerful resource for some of those suffering from severe anxiety. Activities like this can benefit people that feel overly worried and scared about an upcoming test, a significant lecture, or an important event.

HOW DOES EXERCISE HELP EASE ANXIETY?

Participating in the exercise is a distraction away from the exact thing you 're nervous about.

Moving the body reduces muscle tension, reducing the body 's contribution to feeling nervous.

Raising the heart rate affects brain chemistry, increasing the availability of essential anti-anxiety neurochemicals, like serotonin, gamma-aminobutyric acid (GABA), brain-derived neurotrophic factor (BDNF) and endocannabinoids.

Exercise stimulates the frontal cortex regions responsible for executive function, helping to regulate the amygdala, our system 's reaction to real or perceived threats to our survival.

Exercise periodically builds up tools to improve endurance against stormy emotions.

So how much exercise does someone need to guard against episodes of people with anxiety disorders? Although this not easy to classify, a meta-analysis in the journal Panic-Depression discovered that employees with mental illnesses who reported high-level physical exercise were better shielded from symptoms of anxiety than those who reported low physical activity. Bottom line: more movement is easier when it comes to managing anxiety.

Don't feel bad if you're just starting out. Some work also indicates that a single bout of exercise will help to relieve anxiety when it hits.

The type of exercise you select will not matter very much. Research points to the efficacy of everything from tai chi to high-intensity periodic training. People have encountered change, no matter what sort of operation they have attempted. General physical exercise is good, too. The main thing is to try things out and continue doing them.

MAXIMIZING THE BENEFITS:

- Go for something fun to do regularly, creating resilience.
- Exercise to get the heart rate up.
- Join a friend for a party to enjoy the added benefits of social support.
- If necessary, work out in the natural world or green areas, which further reduces stress and anxiety.

Although scientific studies are relevant, you don't have to check a map, stats, or a professional to realize how good you feel after sweating. Remember these emotions and use them as a reason to do something constructive every day. It's time to wake up and move!

Once you have depression or anxiety, workout often seems to be the last thing you want to be doing. But as soon as you get excited, exercise will make a huge difference.

The exercise aims to alleviate and enhance a variety of health issues, including high blood pressure, diabetes, and arthritis. Evidence on depression, anxiety, and exercise suggests that the physiological effects of exercise can also help to boost mood and alleviate anxiety.

The relationship between depression, anxiety, and exercise is not completely clear — but exercising, and other types of physical activity will undoubtedly relieve the anxiety disorders and improve mood. Exercise will also help prevent depression and anxiety from returning until you feel good.

HOW DOES EXERCISE HELP DEPRESSION AND ANXIETY?

Daily exercise can help to relieve depression and anxiety by:

- Release of feel-good endorphins, natural cannabis-like brain chemicals (endogenous cannabinoids), and other natural brain chemicals that can help improve your perception of good health.
- Take your mind off the stress so you can get away from the loop of negative thoughts that fuel depression and anxiety.
- Regular exercise also has many psychological and emotional benefits. It could support you.
- Gain confidence. Achieving exercise goals or tasks, even small ones will improve your self-confidence. Keeping in shape will help you feel better about your appearance, too.
- Have more social connections. Exercise and physical activity can give you a chance to meet or socialize with others.

Just exchanging a friendly smile or a
greeting while you're walking around
your neighborhood can help your mood.

- Cope safely. A safe coping mechanism is
to do something constructive to treat
depression or anxiety. Trying to feel
good by consuming alcohol, focusing on
how you feel, or believing that anxiety
and depression will go away on their own
can lead to chronic pain.

IS A STRUCTURED EXERCISE PROGRAM THE ONLY OPTION?

Some studies show that physical exercise, such as
normal walking — not just structured exercise
routines — may help improve mood. Physical activity
and exercise are not quite the same thing, but both of
them are advantageous to your wellbeing.

Physical exercise is any exercise that works in
your muscles and involves energy and may include
work or household or leisure activities.

Exercise is a scheduled, organized, and repeated
body movement that is performed to enhance or
maintain physical fitness.

The word "exercise" can make you think of

running circles around the park. But exercise involves a wide variety of activities that improve your level of activity and make you feel better.

Of course running, lifting weights, playing basketball, and other physical exercises that get the heart pounding will help. But so can physical exercise, such as gardening, cleaning your house, walking around the road, or other less stressful activities. Any physical activity that gets you off of the sofa and moving around will help to change your mood.

You don't have to do all the workouts or any other physical activity simultaneously. Expand how you think about exercise and find ways to increase a small amount of exercise all through your day. For example, Use the stairs instead of the elevator, for starters. Park a little further away from work to get in a short stroll. And, if you're living close to your office, explore cycling to work.

HOW MUCH IS ENOUGH?

Undertaking 30 minutes or more of exercise every day for three to five days a week will dramatically boost symptoms of depression or anxiety. Yet smaller amounts of physical activity — just as little as 10 to 15 minutes at a time — may make a significant difference. It can take less time to exercise and boost your mood when you perform more physical exercises, such as running or cycling.

The psychological health benefits of physical exercise can last only if you commit with it in the long term — another valid reason to concentrate on pursuing things that you enjoy.

HOW DO I GET STARTED — AND STAY MOTIVATED?

Beginning and adhering to exercise routine or regular exercise can be a difficult task. These steps may help:

Pinpoint what you're enjoying doing. Find out what kind of physical activity you 're most likely to do, and think about when and how you 're most likely to do it. For starters, will you be more likely to do some kind of gardening in the evening, resume your day with a jog, or go for a bike ride, or play basketball with your kids after school? Do what you like to help you stick to it.

Get the support of your mental health professional. Consult a doctor or mental health expert for support and supervision. Discuss your fitness schedule or physical activity regimen and how it works with the overall recovery plan.

Set a realistic target. Your job doesn't have to be five days a week for an hour. Think critically about what you would be able to do and proceed slowly. Tailor the strategy to your own desires and skills, rather than setting out the unrealistic expectations that you are impossible to follow.

Don't think of intense exercise as a task. When exercise is yet another "should" in your life that you don't think you 're living up to, you 're going to equate it with disappointment. Instead, look at your diet or physical activity schedule the same way you look at your therapy sessions or meds — as one of the resources to help you feel better.

Evaluate the obstacles. Find out what's actually preventing you from being physically fit or getting exercise. For example, if you feel self-conscious, you may want to exercise at home. When you stick to your goals easier with your partner, find a mate to work with or who likes the same physical activity you do. When you don't have the money to spend on fitness clothes, do anything that's cost-free, like exercising on a regular basis. When you think about what's keeping you from getting physically involved or exercising, you may be able to find an alternate solution.

Prepare for delays and obstacles. Give yourself some kudos for every good step, no matter how insignificant it is. If you miss the workout one day, that doesn't mean you can't keep up with the workout regimen and you'd rather quit. Just try it again the next day. Stick the fuck with it.

EXERCISE AS ANXIETY MANAGEMENT

Of course, lack of activity is not the source of distress for everyone. Several people are genetically nervous. Some had experiences that influenced their symptoms of anxiety. Whether or not inactivity exacerbates your anxiety, there is also evidence to assume that exercise alone can be one of the best ways to handle it.

Anxiety treatment is about doing activities that combat anxiety, and exercise – of all possible behaviors – is probably one of the best remedies for anxiety. Proof suggests any of the following:

Working to prevent passivity In the first place, of course, is that exercise is the opposite of inactivity. If you work out, the impact of inactivity on anxiety will no longer be there. Even if your inactivity did not cause your distress, it also makes you worse off. Exercise decreases the risk that inactivity-related anxiety will affect you.

Releasing "Relaxation" Neurotransmitters Now, the main explanation that exercise acts as an effective anxiety treatment strategy is that exercise often has some of the same impacts as certain anxiety drugs. Exercise produces endorphins in your brain, which are the leading painkillers in your body. They are technically free to prevent workout from causing distress, but they also play a significant role in mood regulation and mind relaxation.

Burning Cortisol Almost everyone dealing with anxiety is likely to have surplus cortisol in their body as a result of the burden that anxiety brings on them. Exercise lowers cortisol, eliminating many of the symptoms that contribute to more anxiety, such as attention issues and fatigue.

Improved Sleep Routine often tires the body enough to make it easier to sleep with anxiety-something that many anxiety sufferers are grappling with. Sleep is vital to controlling anxiety, and the ability to exercise to boost sleep is essential.

Healthy exercise is, in general, a useful coping tool. Coping is about making sure you spend time in ways that are good for your mental health, and exercise is certainly a way to do that.

There are many explanations about why exercise can also help with anxiety. Exercise enhances trust. It guarantees that your body is safe and that good health is essential to any mental disorder. It also makes the bodywork more effective and avoids any "misfiring" that may cause chronic anxiety.

But, on the other hand, there are several activities that you don't think will affect anxiety in terms of helping to resolve it.

While any sort of exercise is right for you, some are especially beneficial when it comes to reducing anxiety and improving psychological health.

BEST EXERCISES FOR ANXIETY MANAGEMENT

Here are the best exercises that can help you control your anxiety and make you feel better:

YOGA

With a good cause, this is the most common type of exercise linked to emotional wellbeing. The entire idea of yoga is used in mind-body relation by relaxation and breathing exercises practiced. Not only can this be effective on an immediate basis, but it can also have significant long-term consequences, help to alleviate stress and anxiety, depression and frustration, and encourage and improve a feeling of tranquillity.

TAI CHI

The ancient style of exercise from China incorporates the movement of martial arts with meditative movements similar to those used in yoga. Unlike yoga, Tai chi will help to strengthen the relationship between physical and mental wellbeing, helping to encourage a sense of balance and relaxation. The significant components of Tai chi, including mental concentration, physical coordination, muscle relaxation, and synchronized breathing, are all incredibly relaxing and can go a long way to alleviate tension and minimize anxiety.

RUNNING

It is a traditional fitness staple and can be a successful form of workout for those trying to improve their emotional and physical health.

Connection to alleviate anxiety is not difficult to build, as acting or running helps promote the release of endorphins in the body. Such neurotransmitters are responsible for creating a feeling of wellbeing that can be highly helpful in the battle against anxiety and depression.

WALKING

Not everyone is strong enough to run, but most people can walk to exercise. A regular 30 minutes' walk has been demonstrated to lower anxiety and stress and improve your health. You can walk just about anywhere, but you can also find beautiful working places in city parks and state parks. They often have easy walking trails in the surroundings of nature that reduce stress and promote a feeling of peace and balance.

HIKING

Another type of movement that can also induce the production of a hormone, hiking can be as excellent as running when it comes to stress relief. The added benefits here can get out and connect with nature, which can be incredibly useful in terms of relaxing risks and enhance your mood. It can only help you change your immediate environment and get your mind out of your daily problems. It's even better if you can share the hike with your partner and improve your sense with well being even more.

STRENGTH TRAINING

Although most people identify this type of exercise with building muscle, they can do a lot to boost your mental wellbeing. The benefits here come from growing your self-esteem as you begin to feel the tangible results of your workouts. You can see your morale grow as you not only feel better about yourself but also gain a sense of pride as you rack up good results. If you feel happier and spend more time, you will also be able to sleep better, which can also go a long way in preventing anxiety.

DANCING

People don't tend to think of dancing as an exercise, but could have a lot of physical advantages as it aids work out muscles, pump your heart, and even help you shed excess weight. At about the same time, it can help you boost your emotional health by giving you a sense of fulfillment as well as giving you the chance to let go and have some enjoyment. Since dance can be such a beautiful means of self-expression, it can help you get in touch with your emotions and let them out innovatively and soothingly. Besides, if you do something that you love, you 're more willing to comply with it.

Of course, there is no certainty that exercise alone can help you resolve the symptoms of anxiety. Still, it can be a perfect complement to any therapeutic plan because it has so many beneficial benefits. There's almost no downside to integrating exercise into your everyday routine. If you want to start feeling less tired and less and less nervous, why don't you get up and walk to find out what daily exercise can do for you?

Unless you haven't been training for a while, you should start with little and often, and make sure you warm-up and down to help prevent injury—the crucial step in building momentum and develop a habit of exercise.

5

LEARN HOW TO SELF-SOOTHE

*A*nxiety is a reality we all need to deal with sooner or later. And how you support yourself through it makes all the difference in the world.

THE ART OF SELF SOOTHING FOR ANXIETY AND OTHER EMOTIONAL CHALLENGES

Among the first self-help strategies needed to master all of the emotional challenges that we may encounter is one known as self-soothing. The idea of this is so straightforward that you'll ask, "How is something so simple going to help me surmount my depression?" (Or anxiety or whatever you're dealing with now.) It works because it requires the ability to control your moods by relaxing or gratifying yourself in the face of negative emotions such as depression. It means learning to relax without drugs, food, alcohol, or other harmful distractions. It's a compilation of approaches designed to help you deal with strongly negative or anxiety-causing feelings.

This is not a new concept or one of "mental mumbo jumbo." Instead, it is what emotionally productive people learn from childhood that you may have overlooked, mainly if you came from a dysfunctional home. It's a vital skill base aimed at self-preservation that can make a mark of a good and a happy person and a desperately suffering and "stuck" one. I don't think that self-confidence has received enough attention considering how critical it is. And it's possible for both of us.

There are days, and many times, when things may not be as you had expected. As a consequence, you 're feeling bad. In reality, to be blunt, you may feel like absolute garbage.

You might be worried about current or past problems or dreading future activities that would usually cause self-destructive actions or an excessive dose of depression. You may be very nervous, or you might experience an upheaval in your relationships. You may be afraid that you will be betrayed by a partner or a significant other. Those are all times when you are most likely to gravitate back to unhealthy patterns.

You may realize that you are unable to tolerate whatever you feel, and that thought alone may send you to the chest of the medicine, the liquor store, or the cookie bin. You might head out to the city to find a replacement for the loved one, someone to make you feel "special and loved." You'll get an image of all the stupid stuff that we're going to do to thwart the pain. Unfortunately, we all know that these techniques don't work; then we end up fat, drunk, discarded, or in another terrible relationship. Then we feel even more distressed than we did before we set out to make ourselves feel better with our brand of self-help.

Whether you're struggling to calm down, have untreated trauma, or have a highly stressed and damaged nervous system, this section of this book will give you a few useful suggestions to learn how to calm down.

WHAT IS SELF-SOOTHING?

Self-soothing is a social, physical, psychological, and biological developmental activity that every child must learn to grow up. Simply put, self-confidence is the capacity to calm down after experiencing something stressful.

There is a lot of controversy surrounding when the time is right for a child to calm down – but eventually, at some stage in our early pre-teen years, self-sustaining needs to happen.

WHY ARE SELF-SOOTHING SKILLS IMPORTANT?

Coping methods are complicated, much like the people who are dependent on them. When it comes to stress and anxiety, it's a good idea to have a few skills available to help you find relief.

For instance, seeking welfare support can be an effective way to boost your mood. However, signs of PTSD, such as painful memories or feelings about a past traumatic incident, can also occur suddenly. These are times when social support may not be readily available.

It's necessary, therefore, to learn the coping mechanisms that you can do on your own.

Signs You Need to Learn Self-Soothing

- You prefer to think about it all

- You're living a hurried and anxious life
- You're struggling to slow down
- You've had panic attacks
- Depression is chasing you all day long.
- You appear to overthink it all
- You're caught in endless loops of thinking
- You are suffering from some trauma
- You feel overwhelmed by the universe
- You are approaching new situations from a place of fear rather than curiosity.
- You feel unloved or abandoned by others;
- You feel detached from your inner self

SELF-SOOTHING PRACTICES FOR BEGINNERS

I'm not going to mention any fancy visualization or meditation methods here, don't worry about that. Self-soothing needs to come naturally, so I strongly encourage you to find out what works for you. You are more than welcome to unsubscribe from the list of suggestions that I will discuss below.

A word of warning: there are safe and unsanitary ways of self-confidence.

Not everything that 'feels good' when it comes to self-confidence is good for you.

Don't use the justification of trying to relax as a way to explain unhealthy behaviors or activities that affect your mind or body. Definitions of negative aspects of self-confidence include food binging, alcohol consumption, opioid consumption, gambling, TV show binging, unnecessary shopping – Do you get the picture?

Here are some healthy and gentle self-soothing techniques that anyone who struggles with anxiety, PTSD, or overly-sensitized nervous systems can use:

SELF-HOLDING

Okay, the word 'self-holding' can sound sophisticated – but it means giving yourself a big bear hug! Self-holding is a technique promoted by Peter Levine (the inventor of somatic experimentation) with the purpose of anchoring and relaxing the nervous system. It's been proven that the hugs are right for you because they release the feel-good hormone oxytocin – and that the hugs are just as successful! And if you feel overwhelmed or you're on the verge of having a breakdown, go to a quiet spot. Sit back, man. Hug yourself, man. Just reflect on what it's like to be kissed and held, and let the feelings sink in.

GENTLE HAND TECHNIQUE

If you feel nervous, irritated, or overwhelmed, close your eyes and concentrate on your body. In which part of your body do you feel the most fearful? Place a gentle hand over that part of your body, just like a mother would over her kids. Gentle hand technique is a self-parenting technique that fits well alongside inner child labor (but that's a whole other worm can). Wait a few seconds or so, and concentrate on your heart, softly resting on your fear. After a minute or so, you may find your fear and anxiety steadily dwindling.

TUNE IN TO WHAT'S GOING ON AROUND YOU

Similar to focusing on one thing around you, you can also opt to concentrate on other things that are going on around you when you start feeling nervous. "Instead of turning inward, turn outward," Whitney says. "Focus on the physical realm as you see it through your sensory organs: note the feeling of the air on your body, observe the noises in the environment (especially the noises of nature, such as birdsong or wind), and feel your feet on the ground and the seat under your ass, holding you up." She says that generally speaking, this sensory awareness can help to slow down your heartbeat and nervous confidence.

CROSS YOUR ARMS, ROCK, DEEP BREATHING

Those who experience anxiety or PTSD may feel fragmented, chaotic, confused, scattered, damaged, or damaged apart. In this condition, it can be challenging to identify your 'edges' and remain in your body. It would help if you used this strategy when activated by something that actively stimulates the nervous system. Crossing your arms helps give you a sense of being enclosed and rocking imitates the sensation of becoming a fetus nestled in the womb (or, if that feels odd, in the arms of a caring parent instead). Pair that with steady and deep breathing, and you have a reliable source of self-confidence.

GET YOUR BODY MOVING!

If some anxiety or stress occurs, an enormous amount of energy is produced in the body as it prepares for battle or flight. To remove some of the excess energy, get the body going. Consider jumping up and down, heading out for a long walk, or jogging on the spot (or around the block). You can like to release the breath using a technique like ujjayi yoga breathing.

INVEST IN A WEIGHTED BLANKET

This self-soothing technique may be a little pricey, but I think it's worth it. If you're struggling with poor sleep (which often comes with anxiety and PTSD), consider investing in your weighted blanket.

Weighted blankets work by applying deep-touch stimulation (DTPS) uniformly around your body that releases pleasant brain chemicals that are necessary for relaxation.

I own a weighted blanket from an Australian company named Neptune Blankets, and I use it to sleep. You should pick the correct blanket depending on your body weight – usually, the best blanket for you depends on 10% of your body weight. There are other brands out there that you can find. There are two great brands:

Another fascinating self-soothing device is the deep pressure jacket. Deep-pressure vests are used for people with sensory processing disorder or autism – but they can also be used for those who are dealing with anxiety. A deep pressure jacket is a vest you put on that tightly compresses your body – close to a hug. If you want a lighter alternative, you can also choose to try a compression vest worn by athletes, such as this one for women (which is sold as a 'trainer corset') or this one for men.

SELF-MASSAGE

When we are nervous, our muscles appear to contract as it is the body's way of entering fight or flight mode. But what happens when anxiety and fear from the background of your life? The response is that muscle contraction starts to develop into deep muscle tension and knots that need to be massaged.

Massage helps to relax your muscles, increase blood circulation, detoxify your body, and revitalize your strength. Unlike embraces, massage requires a pressurized touch that activates happy-hormones in your brain, such as dopamine and serotonin.

You don't need a lot of self-massage – it's just your face. But I do suggest that you get some kind of device because it will make the process a lot more enjoyable. I've got three different massage devices that I'm going to connect to below and explain what they are for:

- Gua Sha Chinese stimulator for squeezing knots that often form in my neck due to stress (this is the exact one I use)
- A deep-muscle relaxation ball for my whole body (I heat up the ball and lean against the wall with it) – this is the exact one I use.
- Electrical massage for easy massage of the neck and shoulder at the end of the day (this is the one I use)

GOOD SLEEP

Healthy sleep is one of the top priorities in the treatment of anxiety and the prevention of anxiety attacks. Scientific studies have shown that human beings need at least 6-7 hours of sleep on average. Studies have also shown that people with anxiety can reduce about 50% of their anxiety by 8 to 10 hours of sleep. It is also beneficial to lower the likelihood of repeated extreme anxiety.

MOVE AWAY FROM OTHERS TO REENTER YOURSELF

Feeling nervous and on the verge of a panic attack doesn't make fun of itself, but when it happens to other people, it's much worse. Place recommends walking away for a couple of minutes. "Step out of the room to calm your mind and give yourself some time to get together," she says. "This way, you'll take a few moments to collect yourself and then feel more confident about the social situation you're in."

PRACTICE SELF-TALK

The way to help you stay calm is by practicing self-talk, says Dr. Klapow. "It's important to use self-talk — to coach oneself during the day to stay focused and engaged, but also to be reasonably calm," he says. "This will help to calm down the nervous system, including the sympathetic system."

Positive self-talk is something that can be practiced and can be highly helpful in controlling the mental and physical symptoms of anxiety. Worrying thoughts can make us feel physically nervous (such as having a pounding pulse, feeling muscle pain or dry mouth) and worrying thoughts can lead to even more anxiety.

You might say to yourself, "here I go again, I am going to panic" when you're about to do something which consumes you with fright. Anxiety may create a revolving circle of a negative thought, with mental anxiety leading to physical anxiety, leading to more mental anxiety, leading to more physical anxiety.

Positive self-talk is a coping mechanism that can actually change the way of being in the world and disrupt this revolving cycle where negative feelings contribute to more physical symptoms.

HOW TO PRACTICE POSITIVE SELF-TALK:

1. DISCOVER WHAT YOU ARE THINKING

It may sound intuitive, but it's hard to really find out exactly what we're thinking when we encounter a lot of thoughts that happen really quickly. A diary sheet of your thoughts can be useful to give you more clarification. You can find freely available models by searching the internet for them. The method of writing a thinking diary will help bring more reflective knowledge to your stream of thoughts.

2. CHALLENGE THE RATIONALITY OF YOUR THOUGHTS

The more depressed you become, the more likely it is that patterns of thought will become more skewed. So, it may be good to doubt your feelings. Could you be exaggerating, for example? And, do you speak in black and white terms? The easy act of writing down your worries and anxieties will also help give you some perspective on your feelings.

3. REWRITE YOUR NEGATIVE THOUGHTS AND MAKE THEM POSITIVE

Your mindset will become less skewed by replacing negative thoughts with positive ones. You can be faced with constructive obstacles on index cards for quick reference or on your computer. Positive mental-statements may be similar to the following; "I can handle anxiety as I have controlled it many times before" or "I learned to cope with that incident and it should be easier next time" or simply, "I know that I am going to be alright"

Thought diaries can be a valuable way to uncover and test secret ideas behind your feelings. After all, there is something behind every thought in your psyche. Tell yourself what's going to be so bad about something going on, or what's that going to mean?

A therapist can help monitor your thought diary and will be able to provide feedback on your distorted thinking. An important way to counter skewed thought is to always pursue proof to support that thinking. For example, how should someone else see a specific situation? This is where the therapist can provide invaluable insights, as they can help you find your thinking errors. Thinking errors (or what is also known as cognitive distortions) can arise when we begin to see it as all in or all out when we cata-strophize when we personalize things that happen to us, or simply when we jump to conclusions. A psychiatrist may also be able to see when you live by set guidelines and when you overuse the words 'will,' 'must', and 'can't.

COPING STATEMENTS FOR ANXIETY

The aim of this is to avoid the thoughts that lead to anxiety and to replace those thoughts with practical, logical thoughts. Once these logical self-statements are practiced and trained, the subconscious takes over, and they occur inevitably. This is a type of gentle conditioning, which means that your brain chemistry (neurotransmission) occurs as a result of your new thought habits.

WHEN ANXIETY IS NEAR

- I'm going to be okay. My emotions aren't always logical. I'm just going to relax, calm down, and it's going to be alright.
- Anxiety isn't dangerous — it's just painful. I'm fine; I'm just going to move on with what I'm doing or find something more fun to do.
- Right now, I've got some feelings I don't like. They're still all ghosts, though, because they're going to vanish. I'm going to be perfect.
- Right now, I have emotions that I don't

like. They'll be over soon, and I'll be all right. Right now, I'm going to be concentrating on doing something else around me.

- The picture (image) in my head is not safe or logical. Instead, I'm going to concentrate on something safe.
- I've interrupted my depressive thinking before, and now I'm going to do it again. I'm getting better and better at deflecting these automatic negative thoughts (ANTs), and that makes me proud.

So I'm getting a little bit of fear right now, SO WHAT? It's not because it was the first time. I'm going to take some good deep breaths and keep driving. This is going to help me continue to get stronger.

STATEMENTS TO USE WHEN PREPARING FOR A STRESSFUL SITUATION

- I did this before, so I know I can do it again.
- Once this is over, I'm going to be happy I

did it.

- The impression that I have about this case doesn't make a lot of sense. This fear is a mirage in the desert. I'm just going to keep on "walk" forward until I get through it.
- It may not sound very easy now, but it's going to be more comfortable and more relaxed over time.
- I believe I have more power over these thoughts and emotions than I have ever expected. I'm going gently to turn away from my old feelings and step in a different, healthier direction

In conclusion, fear does not have to impede our way of life or, at the very least, our way of enjoying it. You don't need to live life with agonizing anxiety, concern, and apprehension. What's the point of living, if we're still in constant struggle with our expectations and values in life? Such challenges are just our inner monsters that live in our subliminal subconscious. It's possible to tame them. Through anxiety hypnosis, one may live life to the fullest without fear or inhibition. After all, we all have the right to live one.

6

BREAK UP WITH CAFFEINE

*C*affeine is the most common and widely used drug in the world. Records have it that 85 percent of the U.S. population consumes some every day.

An important question to ask is whether it is good for us.

According to the National Institute of Mental Health, about 31 percent of U.S. adults may experience an anxiety disorder at some point in their lives. Does caffeine affect — or even causes — anxiety?

Besides, the Diagnostic and Statistical Manual of Mental Disorders (DSM–5)—a guide recognized by the American Psychiatric Association and used by health practitioners to diagnose mental disorders —

lists   the   following   four   caffeine-related
abnormalities:

- caffeine intoxication
- caffeine withdrawal
- unspecified caffeine-related disorder
- other caffeine-induced disorders (anxiety
  disorder, sleep disorder

CAFFEINE AND ANXIETY

Caffeine is a psychoactive agent that activates the
central nervous system (CNS). This everyone knows,
but what is less understood is how it creates the
effect. Also, caffeine does not excite the neurons
(brain cells), but rather prevents the CNS from
collapsing by binding to adenosine receptors, thus
counteracting the sedative effects of that compound.
In other words, caffeine doesn't make you feel alert
and awake, but it keeps you feeling that way.

Imaging experiments have also shown that
caffeine enhances blood flow in the brain compared
to non-caffeine, where it is much smaller. This
suggests that the slumber encountered is a natural
cycle that is altered by caffeine. The brain is an
expensive machine to maintain in terms of fuel

consumption because it uses about 25 percent of the total energy (glucose) used by the body. It is therefore crucial that the brain conserves as much energy as possible, as it does in different ways. In reality, it would be extremely time consuming and exhausting to examine every piece of sensory information that comes to us. Could you imagine that you're evaluating every person you see? That would have been crazy. So, after all, Mother Nature did a great job, which takes me to my next point: if caffeine stops this usual "slumber" isn't it dangerous to our mental health?

A 2008 study trusted Source demonstrated how caffeine enhances alertness by disrupting a brain chemical (adenosine) that makes you feel sleepy while at the same time activating the release of adrenalin that is proven to increase strength.

When the level of caffeine is high enough, the effects are higher, resulting in caffeine-induced anxiety.

Although there are mental benefits to caffeine, high doses of Trusted sources are known to cause anxiety symptoms, and people with panic disorder and social anxiety disorder are particularly susceptible.

CAFFEINE IS NICE BUT OVERRATED

The beneficial effects of caffeine are valid and essential, but more is not better in this situation.

The behavioral effects of caffeine are also completely known at shallow doses. Consuming as little as 40 mg of caffeine will increase your concentration, alertness, resilience, and reaction time. In reality, higher doses of caffeine may be counterproductive from efficiency or mental performance: after a particular stage, more caffeine can trigger nausea, jitters, and brain fog, and an increase in the amount of energy it generates will make it difficult to remain.

To give you some background, here is the amount of caffeine in some popular beverages recorded by the Center for Public Interest Science:

- One strong (12 oz.) Starbucks coffee, Pike Place Roast: 235 mg
- One cup of ground coffee, House mix, blended with two tablespoons of coffee: 60–80 mg
- One 8 oz. Tasse of distilled green tea: 29 mg
- One 20 oz. Diät Coke: 76 mg
- One 8 oz. Red Bull: 80 mg of

- One of two oz. 5 – Hour Power (or one caplet of Vivarin or NoDoze): 200 mg

Improving physical output requires higher doses of caffeine. Improvements in endurance start taking place at doses of 3 mg per kilogram of body weight, and often, even more, is required. Because most people weigh between 40 and 100 kg (1 kg = 2.2 lbs), a minimum of 120 to 300 mg of caffeine is required to help with distance travel.

Enhancements in strength and power need much higher dosages, and several studies have shown that caffeine will not contribute to any improvement. One literature review showed that 11 of 17 studies found a link between caffeine and power improvement, and 6 of 11 research reported that caffeine was correlated with ultimate strength. Of the studies that demonstrated the advantage of caffeine use before resistance training (weightlifting), the minimum dose required was often at least 3 mg per kilogram of body weight, and often as high as 6 mg/kg.

However, most people do not know that the physical effects of caffeine are primarily due to the placebo effect. So strong is this influence that the higher, the more caffeine subjects say they drink. There is not even a possible physical mechanism by which caffeine can increase strength and power — it works merely mainly by improving your determination so that you drive yourself harder, which you might theoretically train yourself to do without caffeine.

Studies often generally find a more significant advantage to the use of caffeine early in the morning, as it works partially by eliminating any residual sleepiness from the night before.

As you can see in a minute, this only requires 100 mg or so a day to keep getting addicted to caffeine. With this in mind, use is best confined to tiny doses, taken early in the morning, and with an eye to behavioral rather than physical benefits.

ANXIETY SYMPTOMS AND CAFFEINE SYMPTOMS

According to Harvard Medical School, caffeine use can mimic anxiety symptoms.

Caffeine-induced symptoms that may indicate anxiety include:

- Nervosity
- There is restlessness
- Sleeping problems

- Fast heart rate
- Stomach problems

COFFEE AND ANXIETY – HOW CAFFEINE AFFECTS ANXIETY TREATMENT

Coffee and anxiety – how do they respond to each other? Believe it or not, consuming coffee on a daily basis can have a negative effect on anxiety treatment. There is a devastating blow to the mental health behind the pick-me-up strength of caffeine. Read on to learn how caffeine is influencing anxiety.

CAFFEINE TRIGGERS YOUR FIGHT OR FLIGHT RESPONSES

You feel more energized when you drink caffeine. But the energy jolt can also make the body go into a state of panic. A high heart rate signals your mind that something is wrong, causing a fight or a flight response. You feel on the brink, even though there's nothing disturbing about you. Okay, that's not good for the anxiety.

CAFFEINE INCREASES STRESS HORMONES

Many people with anxiety will agree that they have too much tension in their lives — and that caffeine contributes to the pressure.

Caffeine affects the human body much like stress due to elevated heart rate, blood pressure, and stress hormone levels.

Consumption of caffeine may more than double the blood levels of the stress hormones cortisol and epinephrine.

CAFFEINE CAUSES INSOMNIA

Insomnia is one of the most common side effects of both anxiety and caffeine consumption.

In addition, caffeine-induced sleep disorder is a recognized psychiatric condition. If nervous thoughts make you restless at night, the problem can be exacerbated by caffeine.

In particular, caffeine decreases sleep stages 3 and 4 during which intense, restorative sleep takes place.

Adequate, high-quality sleep is one of the most important things you can do for brain health and mental well-being.

Throughout sleep, the brainwashes away toxins and metabolic waste, restores itself, consolidates memories, and develops new brain cells.

Caffeine ingested just six hours before bedtime will dramatically disturb sleep, so you can find that you need to cut caffeine sooner than you expected.

CAFFEINE AFFECTS SLEEP PATTERNS, WHICH ARE VITAL TO ANXIETY TREATMENT

Because caffeine affects the energy levels of your body, it can affect your sleep patterns. You can find it hard to sleep or sleep at night, particularly if you drink coffee all day. Keeping a regular sleep schedule is crucial for the treatment of anxiety and depression and is easier to do without caffeine in your body.

HOW BAD IS CAFFEINE ADDICTION?

Any addictive drug is a hindrance to the treatment of anxiety. Although it may make you feel good for a while, the drug prevents the brain from naturally developing happy chemicals. This refers to cigarettes, leisure products, tobacco, gambling, and, yes, caffeine. The addictive drug also serves as a coping mechanism, stopping you from seeking healthier coping strategies that fix the source of your anxiety.

Like with other habits, caffeine has only gotten worse over time. The body requires more caffeine to satisfy its needs, so you are more dependent on it to get you through the day. Through cutting back on your coffee habits, you will avoid the spread of dependency.

CAFFEINE'S ADDICTIVE POTENTIAL

Consuming as little as 1.5 mg per kilogram of body weight a day is enough to begin to build up a tolerance for caffeine. This means the tolerance should begin to build up at a daily intake of between 70 and 150 mg per day. It's about a cup of coffee a day, or maybe two cups of fairly weak coffee or tea if you're really tall.

When you build up your tolerance, you become dependent on caffeine just to function normally. Effectively, your baseline level of physical and mental activity is lower, so your daily dose of caffeine is just enough to get you back to normal. And if you usually drink 100 mg a day, for example, after a few weeks, you would be subnormal without caffeine: 100 mg will bring you to function normally, but it will take an even higher dose to truly reap the benefits.

If you drink about 750 mg per day — equivalent to 5 to 8 cups of coffee or 15 to 20 cups of tea — your tolerance will be complete. You 're going to avoid having any benefit from caffeine, even at higher intakes. And, of course, the withdrawal is going to be ... not pleasant.

Withdrawal will begin when you normally consume about 100 mg per day. On the positive hand, although the loss of caffeine is unpleasant, it is not dangerous. Interestingly, some of the signs of caffeine withdrawal, much like some of its positive effects, are entirely subjective —caffeine withdrawal does not significantly reduce cognitive ability, even though it almost always feels like it does.

SHOULD I STOP DRINKING COFFEE?

Now that you know the impact of coffee and anxiety, you might be contemplating if you should give up drinking coffee altogether. Every individual has a different tolerance to caffeine. You can be able to take one cup of coffee a day without having any effect on your anxiety treatment. Nonetheless, it can't hurt to reduce the consumption of caffeine.

Start by moving from full-caf to half-caf to half-caf (half the volume of caffeine). And move on to the decaf coffee. You may also turn to black tea, then green tea. Slowly tapering off caffeine reduces the chance of withdrawal.

HOW TO BREAK FREE FROM CAFFEINE ADDICTION

When you start the day off with a cup of coffee or two, get an extra while you're on the drive, an extra after work and an extra to get through the afternoon slump, and maybe a can of pop or candy bar after work followed by ice tea and ice cream after dinner, you may have a severe addiction to caffeine. A lot of people generally feel irritable when the next day's activities close on them at bedtime and are anxious about the next day's problems going through their minds. It's been like this for a few years, with an estimated 80 percent of adult Americans being daily coffee drinkers, and every adult coffee drinker drinking 3.3 cups of coffee a day, without taking into consideration other sources of caffeine.

Medical doctors suggest if you're trying to break off from your caffeine dependence to do it bit by bit but never to try to do it all of the sudden. This will only trigger a caffeine withdrawal to an extreme. There are a lot of ways you can either leave your addiction like a cold turkey, relax, or get help from a professional.

However, the best way to overcome the addiction to caffeine is by knowing that you just have a hard time. When you've got it, you'll be able to conquer your addiction.

HERE ARE A FEW TECHNIQUES YOU CAN IMPLEMENT TO HELP YOU OVERCOME YOUR OBSESSION FOR CAFFEINE:

HAVE A PROPER MENTAL ATTITUDE

If you're in the stage of just considering your desire to avoid drinking coffee, the challenge in front of you may seem very daunting indeed. You may have attempted to leave in the past and failed. What you should bear in mind is that it's possible to conquer your addiction because other people do it every day. This contributes a lot to your quest to stop drinking coffee mind over matter.

AVOID QUITTING COLD TURKEY

One strategy that many people use to avoid coffee is to stop drinking it all at once. I'm not endorsing this form. The explanation is that you may have increased signs of withdrawal, such as insomnia, anxiety, and headache. You also run the risk of overeating caffeine if you have a binge drinking session.

CUT BACK GRADUALLY

When you drink five cups of coffee a day, you can start by cutting it down to four. When you get used to this point, try to cut it down to three, then two, then one or none. I like this slow-down approach because it doesn't induce any shock to your body so that you can suffer much less from painful with-drawal symptoms.

MAKE A CUP OF WEAKER COFFEE

There is nothing more delightful and refreshing than a good cup of strong coffee in the morning. But, if you're trying to nip your coffee drinking habit in the bud, then one thing you can do is add less coffee when you're making your cup. For example, if you are used to adding three tablespoons per cup, then why not start adding two heaping tablespoons and slowly cut it back. Although your coffee is going to be weaker, you can still preserve the flavor to a certain extent by using high-quality coffee.

STOP BUYING COFFEE FOR YOUR HOME

Another brilliant idea is to stop buying coffee when you go to the store. By not taking coffee to your house, you'll be in a much better place to conquer your addiction. One brilliant idea is to avoid drinking coffee at home but only drink it sometimes while you're out with your friends. The advantage of this is that you can love your occasional cup of coffee even more than your usual morning cups.

FIND GOOD SUBSTITUTES

The early evening cup of coffee is a treasured ritual for so many people. There is nothing more soothing than sipping a hot beverage after waking up. One thing you should do is find a suitable replacement. Most people use fruit juice or tea as an alternative. One strategy I knew I would use every day is to prepare a cup of strong black tea with two Lipton tea bags. After I have finished steeping the tea, I add two spoonfuls of sugar and a healthy amount of milk. Sugar and milk help to relieve the acidity of the tea and make it very tasty. I'm still in a position to get my much-needed caffeine fix.

I hope you've found these ideas to stop drinking coffee helpful.

THE ONE-WEEK CAFFEINE ADDICTION SOLUTION

Putting all these details together, here is the exact plan you're expected to follow to kick your addiction in one week.

Before starting: find out what your surrogate habit would be — decaf coffee, herbal tea, root beer, etc. If you usually make or drink your caffeine at home or the workplace, get a supply of your replacement that lasts more than a week. Get a bottle of DL-phenylalanine capsules, too.

The last day you're drinking caffeine: throw out all your caffeine. Coffee, coffee, caffeine pills — get rid of all of them.

Day 1: Consume 1,000 mg of DL-phenyl-alanine first thing in the morning and 1,000 mg about noon. Start consuming your replacement drink instead of your regular coffee beverage at the same time and place that you would usually consume caffeine.

Day 2: Take 1,000 mg DLPA in the morning and 1,000 mg at noon. Day 2 morning is the worst day for most people — once you're out of caffeine that morning, it's all getting more straightforward from there.

Day 3: Take 1,000 mg DLPA in the morning and 500 mg at noon. Around the afternoon of Day 3, if not earlier, the caffeine cravings will be gone.

Day 4: Take 1,000 mg DLPA first thing in the morning and 500 mg at noon. Around the afternoon of Day 3, if not earlier, the caffeine cravings will be gone.

Day 4: Take 1,000 mg DLPA first thing in the morning and 500 mg at noon. Things should be considerably better by this day at the latest: withdrawal symptoms will no longer be apparent, although you are still a few days away from fully resetting your tolerance.

Days 5 and 6: Take 500 mg DLPA in the morning and 500 mg at noon.

Days 7–10: Take 500 mg of DLPA in the morning, but not at midday. By Day 7, your tolerance is likely to be fully reset, and your dependency should be over, but you can keep working for ten days to be positive.

Day 11 and beyond: After ten days, you can start having one coffee beverage a day, in the morning, if you like, as long as it contains less than 100 mg of caffeine. Review this list to find the caffeine content for a drink.

You can also take 500 mg of DLPA in the morning or around noon if you wish. Be mindful that taking it with or shortly before caffeine can improve the effects of caffeine.

RESET YOUR CAFFEINE TOLERANCE

This program is simple and has been proven to be auspicious time and time again. Even for a hot tea drinker like me, it's worth taking a week or two out of caffeine to experience once again the full benefits of the world's favorite product.

Caffeine withdrawal may be painful, but if you follow this procedure, you will only feel moderate pain for the first two days. On Day 3, you 're hardly going to miss caffeine. Within a week or two, your tolerance will be fully reset — it will be as though you've never had caffeine before.

The great news is that you don't have to leave

caffeine forever, so your effort won't be "wasted" if you keep drinking coffee again. In reality, a one-week caffeine wash will allow you to enjoy once again the full benefits of a healthy, low dose of caffeine while still functioning at 100% the rest of the time and sleeping well at night.

7

KEEP UP WITH YOUR DIET

*M*any of us know that eating healthy is essential to our general wellbeing, but what if eating well also improves our mental health? Recent studies have shown that diet can play a role in reducing one's anxiety level.

The nature and composition of the food we eat are under constant scrutiny, and several factors influence our food choices and preferences. The various properties of the food we eat ourselves work in a regulatory feedback system to influence our future choices. One way that food can influence subsequent choices is by affecting mood and, consequently, behavior. Although it is recognized that mood can affect what we eat, here we consider how food affects our mood and, in particular, anxiety levels.

The sugar and fat content of modern diets and refined carbohydrates, in particular, is a high-profile topic for consumer groups, media, and health experts. There are also growing demands from public health authorities and governments to decrease the quantity of fat and sugar in our diet, along with salt. However, these changes may have unintended implications, as our bodies may respond not only to the presence of these compounds in our diets but also to their absence, following nutritional manipulation. Withdrawal of dietary components can affect future food preferences, as well as our mental wellbeing. Generic, carb-restriction, and weight-loss diet plans tend to fail to produce the intended long-term outcomes. Still, heightened interest in the short-term and long-term effects of our diet may increase our ability to successfully adjust our diets to improve both metabolic and emotional wellbeing.

Eating a diet that is well balanced and focused on whole foods versus processed foods is vital. Whole grains, vegetables, and fruits are higher in complex carbohydrates and fiber that help to slow digestion, thereby avoiding significant shifts in blood sugar levels that can contribute to feeling more anxious.

Other strategies include not skipping meals, staying hydrated by drinking adequate amounts of water, and limiting or avoiding caffeine and alcohol. Besides, some studies have shown that specific foods may help to reduce anxiety.

But in the meantime, let's get to the root of the problem by knowing the kinds of foods that trigger anxiety

FOODS THAT CAN TRIGGER YOUR PANIC AND ANXIETY ATTACKS

Let me start by asking you what foods you are sensitive to if there are any? The thing is this that the foods that you are sensitive to, the foods that you consume, eating that food may increase your chances of you having a panic attack. Food does not cause panic or anxiety attacks, but some foods can cause your anxiety levels to be high, and therefore increase the likelihood of a panic attack. What are these foods exactly?

The three food baddies that I am going to look at are caffeine, sugar, and alcohol. Let us look into each one and see how the body reacts to it once it gets into your body.

SUGAR

The kind of sugar I am talking about here is the type that one gets from eating chocolate, maybe a cake or a doughnut. I have nothing against any of these foods, but the truth is they can give you mood swings. Your body moves from having a low sugar level to a high sugar level in a short space of time, and you are brought to a low sugar level again. The high level of sugar does not last in the body because as soon as it enters, the body will release some insulin to try and reduce the amount of sugar in your body. As your sugar levels rise and drop, so you will experience some agitation and get anxious.

If you suffer from panic and anxiety attacks, it would be better for you to get on a low sugar nutrition diet, with vegetables and proteins. Stick to natural sugars derived from fruit.

CAFFEINE

Caffeine is a must for a lot of people to kick-start their day; they have to have that first cup of coffee. Caffeine, however, actually affects the way you're going to be able to cope with stress and all the panic feelings that you may feel during the day. Caffeine makes the body think that there's an emergency that's coming and that's why the body produces adrenaline. And, as we all know, adrenaline causes your heart rate to rise, and when your heart rate is pounding, it raises your anxiety.

ALCOHOL

Alcohol is a stimulant for you. Whatever the state of mind is, with alcohol, it's going to be bigger than it is. Some people who have anxiety may drink alcohol because it seems to have a calming effect on them for a short period. However, alcohol increases the amount of lactic acid in your body, which causes your blood sugar to exaggerate. More than that, alcohol stops you from viewing things logically, and it lets you make the wrong decisions.

NUTRITIONAL STRATEGIES TO EASE ANXIETY

According to the National Center for Mental Health, anxiety disorders are the most prevalent mental disease in the United States. That's 40 million adults—18 percent of the population — who are dealing with anxiety. Anxiety and depression often go hand-in-hand, with about half of those with depression also experiencing anxiety.

Effective treatments and medications can help ease the burden of anxiety, but only about a third of people suffering from this illness are seeking treatment. Through my experience, part of what I'm thinking about when discussing recovery choices is the essential role of diet by helping to relieve anxiety.

In addition to safety recommendations, such as maintaining a balanced diet, consuming enough water to remain hydrated, and restricting or avoiding alcohol and caffeine, other nutritional factors can help to alleviate anxiety. For example, complex carbohydrates are metabolized more slowly and thus help to maintain a more even level of blood sugar, which provides a calmer feeling.

A diet rich in whole grains, vegetables, and fruit is a healthier option than eating a lot of simple carbohydrates found in processed foods. It's also essential when you eat. Don't miss your meals. Doing so may result in a drop in blood sugar that causes you to feel jittery, which may exacerbate your underlying anxiety.

The intestinal brain axis is also fundamental, as a large percentage (about 95%) of serotonin receptors are found in the intestinal lining. Research is examining the potential of probiotics to treat both anxiety and depression.

Make these foods a part of your anti-anxiety diet - You might be surprised to learn that specific foods have been shown to reduce anxiety.

- Magnesium-low diets have been shown to improve anxiety-related behaviors in mice. Foods naturally rich in magnesium can, therefore, help a person to feel more relaxed. Sources are leafy greens, such as spinach and Swiss chard. Specific sources include fruits, nuts, seeds, and whole grains.
- Zinc-rich foods such as oysters, cashews, liver, beef, and egg yolks have been associated with reduced anxiety.
- Other foods, including fatty fish such as wild Alaskan salmon, contain omega-3 fatty acids. Research on medical students conducted in 2011 was one of the first to show that omega-3s can help alleviate anxiety. (The study used supplements containing omega-3 fatty acids).
- A report in the journal Psychiatry Research indicated a correlation

between probiotic foods and a reduction in social anxiety. Eating probiotic-rich foods such as pickles, sauerkraut, and kefir was associated with fewer symptoms.

- Asparagus, commonly considered to be an excellent vegetable. Based on research, the Chinese Government has approved the use of asparagus extract as a natural functional food and beverage ingredient due to its anti-anxiety properties.
- Foods rich in B vitamins, such as avocados and almonds

These "feel good" foods stimulate the release of neurotransmitters such as serotonin and dopamine. They are a safe and secure first step in the management of anxiety.

RULES OF THE ANTI-ANXIETY DIET

These rules have three main functions (all of which lead to decreased anxiety): Help interrupt the sugar and blood sugar roller coaster, reduce inflammation, and repair your gut microbiota.

QUIT SUGAR

Removal of sugar-one of the seven most addictive legal substances-is law number one. "Anyone can benefit from cutting back on or quitting sugar," says Wilson. "But if you're anxious, reducing sugar in your diet is a must." Yes, there have been studies that show a link between anxiety and higher-sugar diets.

That's why Wilson's solution is to fill the negative stuff (sugar) with the good stuff. The tip is consistent with the World Health Organization 's recommendation that adult women eat no more than 6 teaspoons of added sugar per day. (Hint: If you do not know how to find the number of teaspoons of added sugar in a serving, divide the number of grams of sugar.

EAT MORE FOODS WITH TRYPTOPHAN.

Yes, as in the amino acid in turkey that makes you sleepy.

Why? The neurotransmitters in your brain and body are formed from amino acids that you can only get from your dietary protein. "If you don't get enough of these amino acids — especially tryptophan — there's not enough to synthesize serotonin, norepinephrine, and dopamine that can contribute to mood problems, and, indeed, research suggests that this is real. (FYI: serotonin, norepinephrine, and dopamine are all neurotransmitters that are essential for mood regulation).

The easiest way to get tryptophan is to eat three servings of protein, such as turkey, chicken, cheese, soya, nuts, and peanut butter, a day. The only requirement is to aim for grass-fed or free-range animal products, if possible, as grass-fed meat has been shown to have higher levels of omega-3s, which minimize inflammation.

FEAST ON FISH.

Studies have shown that one of the most prevalent nutritional deficiencies in people with mental illness is the lack of omega-3 fatty acids, Wilson says. We still don't know whether this omega-3 deficiency is the cause or effect of mental problems, but it suggests adding long-chain fatty acid-rich fish such as anchovies, herring, salmon, and trout to your diet two to three times a week. (If you are vegetarian, these meat-free foods offer a healthy dose of omega-3 fatty acids.)

PRIORITIZE FERMENTED FOODS.

You've probably learned right now that fermented foods contain good-for-your-good probiotics. But do you know that one study found that those who consume fermented food have fewer symptoms of social anxiety? That's why Wilson recommends eating one cup of full-bodied plain yogurt or 1/2 cup of sauerkraut every single day. (Note: Some sauerkraut is only pickled in vinegar, so make sure that it is really fermented if you're buying kraut from the store.)

SUPPLEMENT WITH TURMERIC.

Turmeric is known for its anti-inflammatory effects. That's why Wilson recommends eating 3 teaspoons of ground turmeric a day. (Here are some of the health benefits of turmeric).

"The best way to eat turmeric is with a source of calories like coconut oil for bio-availability and black pepper which helps with digestion," she says. This guide on how to add turmeric to almost every meal can help you get the most out of the spice.

SO, DOES THE ANTI-ANXIETY DIET WORK?

Basic recommendations – consume no sugar, but prioritize tryptophan, turmeric, healthy fats, seafood, fermented foods, leafy vegetables, and bone broth – seem simple and safe enough. Yet will their follow-up really help to reduce anxiety? In fact, according to other experts, it could.

What are some foods to ease your anxiety?

Fatty fish

Fats such as salmon, mackerel, sardines, trout, and herring are rich in omega-3. Omega-3 is a fatty acid that has a positive association with both cognitive performance and mental wellbeing.

However, recent research has shown that if someone overeats another fatty acid, called omega-6, and not enough omega-3, they may increase their risk of developing mood disorders, such as anxiety.

Omega-3-rich foods containing alpha-linolenic acid (ALA) have two essential fatty acids: eicosapentaenoic acid (EPA) and docosahexaenoic acid (DHA).

EPA and DHA regulate neurotransmitters, minimize inflammation, and promote healthy brain function.

A longitudinal study of 24 people with substance abuse disorders showed that EPA and DHA supplementation resulted in lower rates of anxiety. However, further work is required.

Current guidelines advise eating at least two servings of fatty fish each week. A study of men found that consuming salmon three days a week decreased self-reported anxiety.

Salmon and sardines are among the few foods that contain vitamin D.

VITAMIN D

Researchers increasingly relate vitamin D deficiency to mood disorders such as depression and anxiety. A report in the Journal of Affective Disorders believes that there is sufficient evidence to show that vitamin D is a definite aid to depression. Many studies on pregnant women and older adults have also shown how vitamin D may improve mood. Vitamin D can also boost seasonal disaffected conditions (SAD) during the winter months.

EGGS

Egg yolks are another essential source of vitamin D.

Eggs are also an excellent source of protein. It is a complete protein, meaning that it contains all the essential amino acids that the body needs for growth and development.

Eggs also contain tryptophan, an amino acid that helps to produce serotonin. Serotonin is a chemical neurotransmitter that helps to control mood, sleep, memory, and behavior. Serotonin is also believed to improve brain function and to alleviate anxiety.

PUMPKIN SEEDS

Pumpkin seeds are an excellent source of potassium that helps control electrolyte balance and maintain blood pressure.

Eating potassium-rich foods, such as pumpkin seeds or bananas, can help to reduce symptoms of stress and anxiety.

Pumpkin seed is also a good source of the mineral zinc. One analysis of 100 female high school students showed that zinc deficiency could have a detrimental impact on mood.

Zinc is essential for the growth of the brain and

nerves. The largest zinc storage sites in the body are affected by emotions in the brain regions.

DARK CHOCOLATE

Researchers have discovered that chocolate can help relieve tension.

Scientists have long suspected that dark chocolate might help to reduce stress and anxiety. A 2014 study found that 40 g dark chocolate helped alleviate perceived tension in female students.

Other studies have generally shown that dark chocolate or cocoa can improve mood. However, many of these studies are retrospective, so the findings should be viewed with caution.

While it is still unclear how dark chocolate reduces stress, it is a rich source of polyphenols, especially flavonoids. One study suggested that flavonoids may reduce neuroinflammation and cell death in the brain as well as improve blood flow.

Chocolate has a higher tryptophan content that the body uses to convert into mood-enhancing neurotransmitters, such as serotonin. Dark chocolate is a good source of magnesium, too. Eating a diet with plenty of magnesium or taking vitamins may reduce the symptoms of depression.

When choosing dark chocolate, aim at 70% or more. Dark chocolate also contains added sugars and fats, so a small portion of 1 to 3 grams (g) is sufficient.

TURMERIC

Turmeric is a spice widely used in Indian and South-East Asian cooking. Curcumin is the active ingredient in turmeric. Curcumin can help reduce anxiety by minimizing oxidative stress and inflammation that often increases in people with mood disorders, such as anxiety and depression. In a 2015 study, curcumin reduced anxiety in obese adults.

Another study found that an increase in curcumin in the diet also increased DHA and reduced anxiety. Turmeric is natural to add to your meals. It has a limited taste, so it goes well with smoothies, curries, and casserole dishes.

YOGURT

Yogurt contains good bacteria, Lactobacillus, and Bifidobacteria. There is growing evidence that these bacteria and fermented products have beneficial effects on the health of the brain.

According to a recent clinical review, yogurt and other dairy products may also have an anti-inflammatory effect on the body. Some research suggests that chronic inflammation can be partly responsible for anxiety, stress, and depression.

Adding yogurt and other fermented foods in the diet may benefit natural intestinal bacteria and may lessen anxiety and stress.

Fermented foods include cheese, sauerkraut, kimchi, and fermented soy products.

GREEN TEA

Green tea contains an amino acid called theanine, which is under increasing scrutiny due to its remarkable effects on depressive disorders. Theanine has anti-anxiety and soothing effects and may stimulate the volume of serotonin and dopamine.

Green tea is simple to add to your daily diet. It is an appropriate substitute for soft drinks, coffee, and alcoholic beverages.

While more work is required to investigate the relationship between food, mood, and anxiety, it might be helpful to pursue a healthier diet in addition to any treatment or therapy recommended by your doctor.

Besides, diet plays an incredibly important role in ensuring that we live a disease-free life. The same applies to diet and anxiety-related disorders. Most people have bad eating habits and drink food that can make their anxiety worse.

To begin with, one must always ensure that he/she obtains the right amount of water. Water is 60 percent of our body weight and is essential for the body's metabolic processes. The lack of water will lead to dehydration. The dehydrated condition causes a person to feel exhausted and lethargic, which in turn can lead to an inability to focus. Adequate hydration often means that we are continually energized and able to perform tasks.

Secondly, caffeine-rich foods, such as coffee and its derivatives and energy drinks, should also be avoided. Caffeine helps to induce short spurts of energy and keep us from feeling sleepy. Nonetheless, we continue to feel lethargic as soon as its effects come to an end. Besides, caffeine helps to suck water out of our bodies, making us vulnerable to dehydration. Palpitations, a common symptom of anxiety may also be caused by caffeine.

The value of a well-balanced diet should not be underestimated. A nutritious diet will ensure that we obtain all the necessary macro and micronutrients in sufficient quantities. This ensures that the synthesis of hormones and chemicals can be performed within the body. Fruits and vegetables are rich in vitamins and minerals that are important to fight disease and stress.

A diet that is well balanced and nutritionally full does not fully help or cure us with anxiety. However, its advantages go a long way to ensuring that we stay safe and free from disorders that predispose us to anxiety.

8

TALK ABOUT YOUR WORRIES

*C*an you share your concerns with a friend to help you solve your problem and be more productive?

Worrying alone does not have to be toxic, but it tends to become toxic because we lose perspective in isolation, Hallowell told Science of Us blog. They prefer to globalize, to catastrophize because no one is there to serve as a reality check. Our imaginations are running wild.

Speaking to others makes you look at problems in a different light and find answers. Have a cup of tea with someone who's taking care of you or give them a call. Let them know you're not alright.

Talking things out will help to ease your anxiety

and convince you that there is a more substantial or different way forward.

You don't have to be harsh or try to fight issues by yourself.

Problems and problems can be hard to come to grips with when they're all running around inside our heads.

Sometimes you might expect people close to you to know that you don't feel right. You may feel they should know what you're going through. But, maybe they haven't heard, or maybe they're waiting for you to inquire, not wanting to interrupt.

When you express your thoughts to them, people are always able to support a friend in need. Your friends or relatives are going to be happy, you asked. We would also feel fortunate to be asked to do so in the first place.

WHY TALKING ABOUT OUR PROBLEMS HELPS SO MUCH

There's more to the age-old advice to just "talk it out" than it seems. Here's some evidence that shows why it's so helpful.

When your car breaks down, either you know how to repair it, or you know how to find someone who can do it. Emotions, on the other hand, are a little harder to repair. There's no wrench that you can pick up or a repair shop that you can take your feelings to. Yet you have one device in your arsenal that you can still use: chat about your feelings. Even talking to someone else about your feelings out loud will help. So why are we avoiding it or believing that it doesn't work?

There are a lot of reasons why it can be challenging to think about our problems. Some people (especially men) are socialized to internalize feelings, rather than to give them a voice. Often the very feelings you're struggling with — like remorse about anything you've done, or embarrassment about how you think you're perceived — may feel so daunting that you can't get the strength to talk it out.

No matter why you hold it in, communicating has critical psychological benefits that may not be apparent. "Talking about it" is a specific term, though, so let's explain it a bit. If we think about your issues, it may take a few forms such as:

Venting to a trusted friend-Sometimes, you need to let out how you feel with no clear strategy for a solution. "I've had the worst day at work. "It can be the start of a dialogue that will help you relieve the tension of a long day.

Discussing a conflict with a partner-Fights is going on in relationships, but keeping your feelings to yourself can cause issues to fester between you and your partner. While working on meaningful solutions to your relationship issues is always a positive thing; to be honest about your feelings with your partner will also make your interactions better.

Talk counseling with a licensed therapist-There's a reason people are paying money to talk about issues with a therapist. If you need to address a mental disorder that you're dealing with, are counseling partners to work on your relationship, or just need someone to talk to who knows how to cope with stress, a good therapist will help you get rid of your emotions.

Being honest about your struggles-Sometimes venting to no one, in particular, will benefit not only you but others as well. For starters, in 2015, Sammy Nickalls, a blogger, launched the social media hashtag #TalkingAboutIt to empower people, to be honest about their mental disorder challenges. The act of sharing what daily life is like can help you and others with the same struggles realize that you're not alone and that what feels overwhelming is normal.

What all these types have in common is that they are discussions expressly designed to explore and convey the feelings that you have, rather than relying on a concrete answer. It's always important to find out what you can do to change the situation, but verbalize how you feel can be part of the solution as well.

WHY DOES TALKING ABOUT IT HELP?

Getting a new job, having to break up with a terrible partner, or investing in your self-improvement are all practical things you can do to solve your life's problems. But what's the point of just talking about it? When you fight the frustrating uphill war against your own negative emotions, it can seem like thinking about it is the least useful thing you can do.

In reality, your brain and body get a lot out of talking.

When you feel very intense feelings — especially fear, aggression, or anxiety — your amygdala is running the show. This is the part of the brain that, among other things, controls your fight or your flight response. It's up to the amygdala, and your limbic system as a whole, to find out whether anything is a threat, to formulate a response to that danger whether possible, and to store the details in your memory so that you can remember the danger later.

When you get anxious or frustrated, this part of your brain can take over and even bypass more rational thought processes.

Research from U.C.L.A. suggests that putting your feelings into words — a process called an "affect label"—may reduce the response of the amygdala when you encounter things that are upsetting. That is how, over time, you will become less worried about something that worries you. For example, if you were in a car accident, even sitting in a car directly after that could overwhelm you emotionally. So when you think about your experience, put your emotions into words and analyze what happened, you can get back in the car without getting the same emotional response.

Research from Southern Methodist University suggested that writing about trauma or talking therapy has had a positive impact on the health and immune system of the patient. The study argues that it is stressful to hold back thoughts and emotions. You've got negative feelings either way, but you've got to work to repress them. This can task the brain and the body, making you more vulnerable to getting sick or just feeling bad.

None of this is to say that thinking about your issues or just thinking to a licensed therapist will immediately solve everything and make you happy and safe right away. Nonetheless, like eating healthy and exercising more, it will help improve your overall well-being. Most importantly, it will help you understand how and why you act the way you do so so that you can handle your feelings most efficiently in the future.

HOW TO GET STARTED

Speaking about your emotions is a symbol of your power. It shows you are in a position to take control of your life. But it can be challenging to know how to start a conversation about your feelings or concerns.

Find the right time to talk as you want to have time to talk and not to be interrupted.

You might find it easier to start a conversation when you do something else. For starters, go out for a walk or do the dishes together.

WHO TO TALK TO

It's a good first step to talk to people we meet. Although you may not be able to talk to friends in person during the lockdown, you should be able to make time for a virtual chat.

Tell someone you know, such as your partner, family member, relative, or neighbor. People will listen and help you if you let them know how you feel. This could also support the people you care for. When you give up your emotions, they could do the same thing. Just being in the company of other people will help.

What if I don't want to talk?

Writing about problems and how we feel helps to make things clear to our minds. Sometimes this is enough to reduce the size of your worries.

You could try to write:

- A message to you on what's going on
- A private blog;
- It's an album
- A poem;

WHY TALKING ABOUT YOUR PROBLEMS IS GOOD FOR YOU

If you've never been to counseling or seen a psychologist on a regular basis, you might wonder why thinking about issues is good for you. There are a lot of benefits to being in contact with your feelings. Speaking about your feelings will improve you, your career, and your relationships.

HEALING YOUR RELATIONSHIPS

You may find once you begin talking through situations that bother you, your life will become easier. You will be able to let go of confusing emotions and healing can begin.

MAKING ROOM FOR POSITIVE THOUGHTS

People are sometimes scared to be honest about feeling sad or in pain because they fear the uncomfortable emotion will grow if brought into the light. If you disregard your emotions, it's going to happen with your acts. Individuals who have issues tend to withdraw from others or not be vigilant when they spend time with others. This can hurt relationships with family and friends. Also, it is dangerous that people behave improperly in social settings because they are unable to regulate their emotions.

Although there are many advantages of thinking about your issues, one of the key reasons is that you can't fix your issues until you tackle them. Recognizing the concerns is the first step towards addressing internal disputes and related issues. If you allow yourself to feel sadness, even if you have pain, you will make room for positive thoughts. Talking about your problems is good for you because expressing pain can help to ease the suffering.

Also, many turn to self-medication to "deal" with problems, but doing so doesn't address the issue, it just masks it. Thinking about problems is good for you, so you can deal with real issues through therapy. Doing so will help to minimize the need for self-medication. Choosing to push beyond traumatic events in your life, you 're going to be able to live more entirely.

CHANGING NEGATIVE THOUGHT PATTERNS

It's important to find ways to communicate your emotions, both positive and negative. Sharing good experiences can help you enjoy life to the fullest and thinking about your issues can help you free up stress and anxiety, resulting in healthier choices and happier relationships.

Take the time and you'll find there are a lot of benefits to thinking about your problems. Helpful ears help you learn how to get away from circumstances that can cause you stress or frustration, change negative ways of thinking, and concentrate your attention on your life as a whole, and see the constructive potential for progress.

TALKING ABOUT PROBLEMS IS GOOD FOR YOU

It can be a great relief to seek support. You 're going to build a support system. Find a counselor who you can trust and schedule times to speak on a regular basis. Sharing your stories is an important step towards healing, and if you find that talking about issues is good for you, you may find that you want to build more relationships. If so, your counselor should be able to refer you to a support group attended by people with similar issues.

HOW CAN WE DO IT BETTER?

What is crucial is that not every form of speaking out loud about problems can help. Multiple studies examining college students, young women, and working adults suggest that co-rumination — or consistently focusing on and talking about negative experiences in your life — may have the opposite effect, making you more stressed, and pointing out how great a problem is bothering you. There are a few main things you can do to speak more constructively about your problems.

CHOOSE THE RIGHT PEOPLE TO TALK TO

When you've ever spoken about how you feel, and it feels like you don't get anything out of it, you may be talking to the wrong person. Finding a trustworthy friend who will encourage you (without encouraging bad habits like co-rumination) will help. If you need practical guidance on a problem, find someone who has encountered similar problems and, hopefully, has solved them. And if you need a lot of talk time, try to spread your conversations to many men. One person can get worn out, and having a broad social support system allows you to distribute that burden.

CHOOSE THE RIGHT TIME TO TALK.

It's just as important as choosing who to talk to when you talk to them. Your friends may want to support you, but they have a life of their own. Asking if they have time and energy to chat about before you unpack your emotional bags will help you both get better prepared for a conversation. It also means being courteous about their time. Crises often happen, so you may need to interrupt someone, but most productive interactions can wait.

Seek a doctor, even though you are not mentally ill. Therapists often have the reputation of being necessary only if you have a mental illness. That is not the case. You should go to therapy if you feel overstressed, if you don't sleep well, or if you just want someone to talk to—talk of it less like seeing a doctor, and more like a personal trainer. Also, remember that just like the doctors, mechanics, or anyone else you hire, there are good ones and bad ones (or bad ones for you), so if you don't have success for the first time, try someone else.

GIVE YOURSELF AN ENDPOINT

Not all conversations about your problems need to lead to a plan of action for tangible change, but they do need to lead to more than more complaints. Give yourself space to vent your feelings and, while doing so, focus on how you feel throughout the process. Unless you're trying to get more work done, take a break. If you find yourself thinking about the same stuff over and over without any new insight or relief, seek something else to express the way you feel. You may not be able to fix the external issue that concerns you, but the objective should at least be to change your mood.

TALK ABOUT THE GOOD AS WELL AS THE BAD

It's healthy to express how you feel. Expressing yourself when you don't feel bad. If you're talking to friends, partners, or social media, make sure to share your positive memories and emotions as they come up. Thinking about these interactions will cement them in your subconscious and make it harder to break out of negative thought habits later. Besides, it lets you develop relationships with people you 're close enough to talk to.

Of course, this process can still be a mess. Most days, thinking about your issues may only be moaning about everything that happened at work, but others may be crying in someone's arms for an hour. It can feel embarrassing or uncomfortable the first few times, but the more you open up, the easier it will get to share how you feel.

Holding emotional distress locked within yourself can lead to severe mental health issues or even suicide; you need to speak freely about any difficulties you have to relieve your mental stress.

Whatever the problem you might have, you'll be shocked by how many many people have been in almost the same position as you have. So, if you're concerned about it, note that thinking about your problem is a huge step towards fixing it.

9

MEDITATE AND BREATHE DEEPLY

*A*t some point or another, everybody gets nervous. Typically speaking, being nervous is not an illness – it is a natural anxiety that is connected to fear for the future. Yet when fear affects our behavior and our mental state, that's anxiety. Some people 's anxiety is unpredictable and overwhelming; it can take the form of panic attacks or other "tide wave" reactions. Because it takes up so much of our mental space, anxiety can harm our careers, relationships, and social life. Luckily, anxiety therapy will help people cope with this challenging condition.

Individuals are gradually turning to mindfulness therapy to handle health problems, and schools and hospitals provide meditation courses.

Meditation does help relieve anxiety, depression, and pain, according to 47 reports reviewed in JAMA Internal Medicine on Monday. Still, it does not seem to help with other issues, including drug abuse, sleep, and weight.

We have modest confidence that mindfulness practices have a beneficial impact, wrote Dr. Madhav Goyal of the Johns Hopkins School of Medicine in an email to shots. He says the positive impacts on anxiety, depression, and anguish can be moderate, but they can be seen all over numerous studies.

THE SCIENCE OF MINDFULNESS FOR ANXIETY

Tens of thousands of people have completed the 8-week MBSR workshop since Dr. Jon Kabat-Zinn founded the Mindfulness-Based Stress Management Program at the University of Massachusetts Medical Center in the 1970s. Research shows that, in addition to successfully minimizing stress, MBSR also provides many other mental and physical health benefits, including the potential to help control chronic pain, depression, and anxiety. Evidence is rising that Meditation can help combat depression.

The authors of the study entitled "The Effect of Mindfulness-Based Therapy on Anxiety and Depression: A Meta-Analytic Review" looked at 39 studies involving more than 1,000 participants suffering from a range of clinical conditions, including anxiety. Based on their observations, they concluded that mindfulness-based therapy was a successful and "promising intervention in the treatment of anxiety and mood disorders in clinical populations." They wrote that "The fundamental concept underlying mindfulness activities is that observing the present moment in a non-judgmental and open way can effectively mitigate the effects of stressors because of excessive orientation towards the past or future when dealing with anxiety and depression

HOW MEDITATION WORKS FOR ANXIETY DISORDER

Mental disorders are more than usual anxiety that we may experience when we need to have a speech, have an exam, have a job interview, or get away from parts unknown. For those who have an anxiety disorder, anxious feelings don't go away – they may get worse with time.

With daily anxiety, Meditation is a great help;

with persistent depression, some therapy – for example, mindfulness-based therapy – is recommended. Having some quiet time to breathe deeply and to oxygenate the body will help bring about a calming response. The American Institute of Stress recommends that abdominal breathing be most beneficial for 20 to 30 minutes a day. Breathing exercises make you feel close to your body — bring your thoughts away from the stresses in your head and keep your mind calm.

Instead of thinking about future events and allowing nervous thoughts to overtake you, you should turn to Meditation. Meditation calms your muscles and allows you to enjoy the here and now. And you don't need a special meditation kit to sit down. A few peaceful, reflective minutes in the corner of your home, office, library, school, or park can make a difference. The beauty of Meditation is that it's fully available.

During mindfulness meditation, you pay attention to your breath, visual cue, or physical sensations. Through breath, for example, the sensation of inhalation and exhalation is the focus of your Meditation. Your mind is going to wander, and this is entirely normal. Just try to redirect your focus back to your breathing when you notice it. Remember that you're not messing with or observing the air – you 're just watching it with your full attention.

With time, you will notice that when your mind is calmly settled on the breath – even if it's only for a minute or two – you will experience calmness even though anxious thoughts may pop up like popcorn. That is because once you have learned to understand these nervous feelings, you will let them go slowly but firmly and go back to breathing.

THE EFFECT OF MEDITATION ON OUR MIND - THREE MEDITATIONS FOR ANXIETY

Anxiety doesn't just think negatively, and it also affects the brain's structure and function. Decreases the scale of the hippocampus, the portion of the brain known to be the center of the memory.

Conversely, it increases the amount of the amygdala, the brain area responsible for the response of fear, making you even more anxious and fearful.

Stress, fear, and anxiety trigger stress hormone releases and cause imbalances in neurotransmitters, chemicals that brain cells use to communicate with each other.

It has been known for thousands of years that

meditation can help you relax, but meditation does a lot more than that.

Meditation, like anxiety, changes the structure and function of your brain — but for the better.

A regular meditation practice not only can reduce anxiety symptoms, but it also can reverse the damage caused by anxiety.

With the latest neuroimaging techniques, these changes can be tracked and measured. Researchers from Johns Hopkins University sifted through over 18,700 mindfulness meditation studies to determine its most productive uses. They concluded that the number one use for meditation was anxiety relief.

Meditation, like anxiety, changes your brain's structure and function — but for the better.

Regular meditation practice can not only reduce the symptoms of anxiety but can also reverse the harm done by anxiety.

Such improvements can be monitored and calculated with the new neuroimaging techniques. Researchers at Johns Hopkins University have conducted over 18,700 mindfulness meditation studies to determine its most productive uses. They found that the number one meditation use was anxiety relief.

Here are some of the critical ways in which

meditation strengthens the brain and mental health-being:

1. MEDITATION BREAKS ANXIOUS THOUGHT PATTERNS

The primary way that meditation helps anxiety is by breaking negative patterns of thought.

As anyone with anxiety will attest, racing thoughts are creating a vicious cycle of worry and anxiety. Breaking the vicious cycle of obsessive, negative thinking is where meditation shines.

Meditation can reduce rumination, even in people with long-term mood disorders. It reduces the tendency to worry and improves your control over random, unwanted thoughts.

Meditation can change the way your brain responds to stress.

Every habit is hard to break due to the dominant neural pathway produced by continuous repetition.

And few habits are harder to break than negative self-talk patterns. Many of us have about 70,000 thoughts every day, and 70% of these thoughts are negative.

Fortunately, the brain has an infinite ability to alter, a trait known as neuroplasticity.

Meditation teaches you to take a neutral perspective on your feelings. You learn to recognize and stop "mind time travel"—to worry about the future and to think about the past.

Instead of chasing a troubling thought down the path of all potential negative consequences, you learn to accept it for what it is — one thought — and then let it go, and by forming a new way of thinking, you train the brain to be less nervous.

MEDITATION BALANCES BRAIN CHEMICALS

There is also evidence that anxiety can be caused by brain chemical imbalance caused by severe or prolonged stress.

The practice of meditation will help restore the correct balance of neurotransmitters.

Meditation raises the level of GABA (gamma-aminobutyric acid), a neurotransmitter that is important for feeling happy and comfortable.

Feeling anxious, easily excessively-stimulated, and frustrated are common signs that you may be low in GABA.

Meditation will improve the mood by increasing

the amount of serotonin, another neurotransmitter essential to happiness.

Meditation also decreases cortisol, a stress hormone that contributes significantly to anxiety, depression, sleep problems, and loss of memory.

Meditation Builds a Healthier Brain

Meditation will create a more substantial, healthier brain. The brains of people who meditate regularly show measurable increases in the amount of grey matter, the volume of the hippocampus, and the thickness of the cortex.

Conversely, the size of the amygdala, the area of the brain associated with fear, anxiety, and stress, decreases and becomes less reactive.

Meditation enhances blood flow to the brain, strengthens synaptic links between various parts of the brain, and enhances neuroplasticity. It can make you future-proof of age-related mental decline, including Alzheimer's disease.

MEDITATION REDUCES BRAIN INFLAMMATION

Cytokines are chemical messengers that control the immune response. Increased cytokine volumes are responsible for chronic inflammation, including brain inflammation, and are correlated with anxiety, depression, and other mental disorders.

Meditation helps reduce inflammation to the point of altering the secretion of pro-inflammatory genes.

You would expect gene changes to take a long time, but quantifiable changes can be observed after as little as eight hours of meditation.

TOP MEDITATION PRACTICES FOR ANXIETY CONTROL

PRACTICE 1: A SIMPLE MEDITATION TO OVERCOME ANXIETY

People frequently struggle over the idea of acceptance as an alternative to coping with complicated feelings and states of mind. In the mindfulness-based cognitive therapy (MBCT) groups that I lead, this is likely to occur during the fourth or fifth session when participants ask, "How can I recognize this pain? "Or," I want to experience less of these painful feelings, not more! "These reactions reflect the underlying calculation that while trying to avoid or push away negative thoughts and feelings can be exhausting, the strategy has worked in the past, so ... why risk using a different and unfamiliar strategy?

In those times, letting negative thoughts arise in our lives — for the time being — does not mean that we have chosen not to take action. The definition of acceptance, as introduced in the MBCT, is intended to explain the possibility of forming a different relationship to experience, one that is defined by allowing and enabling experience to occur. Allowing uncomfortable feelings to be in consciousness means acknowledging their presence before choosing as to how to react to them. This takes on a strong effort and requires a deliberate movement of attention. Importantly, "allowing" is not the same thing as being idle or passive or powerless.

Denying negative thought is more dangerous for your mental health - The opposite of allowing is quite risky. Being unable to encounter unpleasant thoughts, emotions, or experiences is always the first link in a mental chain that can contribute to the re-establishment of repetitive, conditioned, and vital habits of thinking. You can see this when someone says, "I'm stupid to think like this" or, "I should be strong enough to cope with it." By contrast, shifting the essential attitude to experience, from one of "not wanting" to one of "opening," allows this chain reaction of the usual reactions to be changed at the first link.

Tolerance allows you to work through any negative encounter - The third is that the MBCT activities provide practical ways to maintain an "allowing and letting be" mentality during traumatic experiences. We always "know" theoretically that it would be good to be more compassionate, sensitive, and accommodating of ourselves and what we feel. Still, we have a minimal idea of how to do it. It is unlikely that these capacities will be produced simply by an effort of will. Instead, they need to work through the body with recurrent practice and education to know how things, such as anxiety, can show up as tightness in the chest, or despair as discomfort in the shoulders.

Bringing awareness/consciousness to the stimuli that surround traumatic experiences provides the possibility of learning to respond to these experiences differently at each moment. Over time, this practice of working through the body may make it possible for people to understand, through their experiential practice, that they can have unpleasant experiences and still be all right.

PRACTICE #2: A MEDITATION FOR ANXIETY AND STRESS

Grant yourself about thirty minutes of this kind of mindfulness practice from MBSR specialist Bob Stahl. You can do so in a sitting spot, standing, or even lying down. Pick a good position where you can be satisfied and alert.

- Take a moment to thank yourself for being here — for taking this time to be here, to go back, to your own lives.
- Connect with your mind and body with a gentle check-in: experiencing any feelings, any possessions, any tightness in your body, as well as experiencing in your mood, feeling in your emotions, and just knowing what you're feeling and letting yourself be.
- Now, very gently, taking the consciousness out of the mindfulness check-in, let's turn our focus to the air: to be conscious of the air in the belly, to spread to the inhalation, and to collapse to the exhalation. Breathing in and breathing out with your awareness.

- Breathe all over your body. From time to time, we can find stress, tightness, achiness, and if we can encourage either of these areas to relax, let that happen. It's also important to know that if we're unable to relax, our practice advises us to let it happen. Let whatever sensations flow and resonate wherever they need to go — the same applies to our feelings and emotions, let them be.

- Be kind to any nervous thoughts that emerge with a careful question. When we feel in this body and mind, we may at times tend to experience some anxious thoughts, anxieties, fears, and there are occasions when we may use the practice of mindfulness, study, and investigation to possibly uncover the underlying causes of our fears. When, even after practicing body scanning and mindful breathing, it seems that we continue with certain nervous feelings, now drawing attention to those feelings themselves, to know what is being felt, to feel fear.

- Dive into your feelings of kindness and gentleness. Much like we often place our toes in the water to acclimate slowly, part by part, to the temperature of the bath. We should dip our toes very softly into feeling fear, only knowing what's there, feeling in fear with awareness — there's no need to try and analyze or sort out anything, only feeling in the sense of feeling nervous, afraid, concerned, and letting yourself be. So whatever happens, just as we understand and let it be, this is how we feel in the heart of terror. Just listen to me with such empathy.

- There is no need to force ourselves further than we can manage, but just to work around the edges, to experience discomfort and to remember. When we learn to live with things as they are, we can discover the root causes of our fear and pain.

- And now, gently withdrawing from the practice of mindful inquiry, come back to the breath again. Breathe in and out, sense the inhalation of the belly in the abdomen, and collapse into isolation. Breathing in and breathing out with a

sense of awareness. Just stay present for
every breath, in and out.

Taking a moment to look at your reflections. Just
as we watch the air come and go, we can also begin to
see the very thoughts that we think areas if we were
observing the clouds flying in the sky, as if we were
sitting at the edge of a river just seeing whatever's
flowing downstream. Starting to observe the mind,
and even the thoughts of fear, are nothing but
moving through psychological events, like clouds,
observing all fearful, unpleasant feelings, just mental
events that come and go. Observing the mind, thinking, noticing the ever-changing nature of thought,
just coming, and going. When we become aware of
the emotions and the traps in which we find
ourselves, we will become free.

And now come back to the air gently. Just be
conscious of breathing in and breathing out. Now, as
we begin to end this meditation on working with
anxiety, let's take a moment to consider all those who
are being faced with these emotions, all those who
live with fear, worry — let's extend our good wishes
for healing, for peace, to all those who live in fear.
Let us take these moments to thank you for proac-
tively tapping into your worries and dealing through

them. When we accustom ourselves to our fears, we will not be so overwhelmed by them. May all beings, where they may be, be safe and free, and may all beings be at ease.

PRACTICE #3: MEDITATION FOR INVESTIGATING PANIC ATTACKS

There is no telling when the next panic attack will occur. It might happen when you're out running errands, talking with strangers in the market or the post office. When in public may sound the worst-case scenario for a panic attack, but it's also the point to listen to the mind and body.

A mindful investigation will help you explore what triggers your panic-stricken feelings so that you can get rid of them. Practice these skills the next time you feel the panic that begins to rise:

Take a moment for the exercise of conscientious inquiry:

Before you start, ask yourself if it's an excellent time to discuss your feelings. Are you feeling safe at this time? If you feel safe, go ahead with the next step. If you don't feel comfortable, then it's all right to wait and pursue this activity at a more suitable time, maybe when you've returned to your home's privacy.

Your practice will begin as soon as you tune in and become mindful of your breathing. Wherever you are — running around the city, meeting a friend, standing in line, or walking down the aisle of the market — you carry your breath everywhere, and it is your focal point for maintaining your connection to the present wherever you go. Be aware of your breathing, in and out, feeling the feelings of warmth as you breathe in and coolness as you breathe out, experiencing the rise and fall, in and out of every breath.

Use this moment to remember all the emotions that are with you right now. If you feel out of control, just accept it as a feeling, without putting any information or stories behind it. When you have an uncontrollable fear that you're going insane, accept that feeling without trying to judge or evaluate that feeling. Give yourself permission to recognize and accept the feelings that are coming up and let them be. You might say to yourself: I feel like something terrible is about to happen. I feel like I've lost contact with reality. I feel like I can't trust anybody. Maybe I can't trust myself. Many unrelated feelings and thoughts can come to mind as if I were hungry. I hope he's going to call soon. I 'm curious where I put my to-do list.

Make room at this moment to let these feelings emerge and try to stay with the same emotions and thoughts as they are. Just accept what's right here, without linking yourself or sticking to a single thought or feeling. You may experience a strong urge to resist or fight against these painful and frightening emotions, as may be your habit. We all have a natural tendency to strive for what feels right. In this exercise, you are practicing non-striving: not trying or not trying to shift your thoughts or push them in a different direction. Just let the emotions be precisely what they are. The less energy you spend trying to resist or alter your panic-stricken emotions, the less panic-stricken you can be.

Try to be mindful of your breathing, and to communicate with the here and now again.

A GUIDED MEDITATION FOR OVERCOMING EVERYDAY ANXIETY

- Sit back comfortably and close your eyes.
- Start connecting to your body, making each inhalation and exhalation gradual and deliberate.
- Next, imagine the direction (in relation

to your body) your future is in. Many people might think it's out in front of them, others would think it's out to the right or to the left. That is called your timeline, and this is how your unconscious mind envisions the history, present, and future.

- Imagine that you're floating above your timeline in your head.
- Now, float out into the future for 15 minutes after the successful completion of the case, which you felt you were nervous about, and stop there. Switch and look back at "Now" in your timeline.
- Ask yourself, "Where's the anxiety? "That's right, it's gone now!
- Travel back to "Now" above your timeline, float down to "Now" and open your eyes.
- Now, the test to make sure the anxiety is released. Think about the thing that used to make you nervous and note that there's no more fear.
- Note: if the anxiety is not resolved, make sure you've imagined that the event was

successfully completed in Step # 5.
Repeat it if necessary.

- The strength of this technique is to imagine events that end in a positive way. Things might still not work out the way you expected, but by doing this form of visualization, you can increase the probability of success.

It only takes ten minutes of your day to practice mindfulness meditation. Some meditate for longer periods, and some meditate for shorter periods, but ten minutes is the recommended time to help with psychological problems. Just find a comfortable spot to sit or lie down and close your eyes. Concentrate on every breath. Thoughts are coming up; just watch them. With continued practice, you will learn a lot about yourself and improve your quality of life. Although this form of meditation is really as simple as that, it can help to have a teacher or a course as a beginner, if only for your own confidence.

10

BE GRATEFUL

*H*ave you ever found that certain people seem to be able to keep a reasonably optimistic outlook regardless of what's going on around them? Like everybody else, they can enjoy the good times, but they still seem to be able to concentrate on the positive in the face of some pretty bad incidents. They see the good in bad people, they see the potential in a tough situation, and they respect what they have, even in the face of failure. Would you like to increase your ability to maintain a positive attitude in your life, even in the face of extreme stress?

Luckily, a proper mindset can be developed with a little practice.

It can be challenging to find something to be

thankful for when you are suffering from anxiety. But practicing everyday appreciation will lead to a significant change in your mental and physical health.

Although it won't make anxiety vanish immediately, gratitude will slowly create a new way of thinking that helps to alleviate anxiety over time. Developing appreciation as a practice will also improve your way of life and make you healthier and happier.

WHAT IS GRATITUDE EXACTLY?

Gratitude is a level of gratitude. It includes experiencing and expressing love and happiness for aspects of your life, big or small. When we have anxiety, we always get stuck in our thoughts and, thus, in our heads. With gratitude, you are moving your attention from your head to your hands. This draws you out of anxious thought and back into your body, and into a relationship with the world around you. Cultivating a heart of appreciation links you with the positive quality of life of other people and with life itself.

When you discuss gratitude in your daily life, you don't need to feel like a challenge. It's a good habit that can be nurtured, but it doesn't need to be one more thing you "should" do. In reality, feeling burdened by a new challenge would probably not lead to much gratitude anyway. While we can use tools and techniques to help us interact with feelings of appreciation at first, if we take a moderate approach, it is more likely to become genuine.

WHAT DO GRATITUDE AND ANXIETY HAVE TO DO WITH ONE ANOTHER?

It is assumed (and studies show) that when you have an appreciation, the weight of anxiety is lifted from your shoulders. You can see the positive even in the worst of situations; you can see the light even in the worst of moments.

A fascinating thing about gratitude is that it's inherent, something intrinsic to our culture. And even though we feel like we're somebody who doesn't feel love, we're not as far removed as we would think. With a shift in our mindset and a dedication to practice, we can gently reconnect with this inherent gene of gratitude.

If you have anxiety, it can be hard to feel happiness. Yet appreciation helps to relieve you from your stressful feelings so that you can see past fear and relate to the present moment. Once we're in the present moment, there's a lot less to feel worried about, and a lot more to feel positive about.

While it may begin as a practice, gratitude will gradually become more reasonable. We're learning to tap into a natural answer. Rediscovering appreciation transforms the view of how you see yourself and the world. Although anxiety is feeling strong, gratitude feels small. It moves our attention from all the traumatic and complicated parts of our lives to the ordinary abundance that is accessible at any moment. We have less of a need to monitor the future by appreciating the present. Hence, we're also willing to relax.

THE SCIENCE BEHIND GRATITUDE

Appreciating the functional aspects of life will alter the behavior of our brains. Several studies have also demonstrated appreciation for the release of dopamine. Dopamine feels impressive, and you're going to want to do it again and again. In this case, dopamine functions as a "reward" neurotransmitter. This internal reinforcement is the basis for creating good behaviors. And, when appreciation is practiced, and it feels good, you're going to start doing it more and more.

In a 2009 report, blood flow was studied in different regions of the brain when gratitude was called "Subjects who displayed more appreciation had higher hypothalamus activity." This brain region regulates some of the body's activities, including feeding, drinking, and sleeping. This also influences pain and metabolism.

Gratitude, too, leads to better sleep. According to a sleep analysis performed by the University of Manchester, more thankful people fell asleep earlier and remained asleep longer. Healthy sleep is vital to mental and physical well-being and helps to reduce anxiety. A good night's rest gives our minds time and space to let go and relax for the next day.

HOW CAN GRATITUDE HELP ANXIETY SUFFERERS

The connection between gratitude and anxiety goes far beyond being able to see the best in the circumstances.

1. GRATITUDE CAN REWIRE YOUR BRAIN

Some of the most significant advantages of appreciation and anxiety are that you will remove the other by getting some. Expressing and harnessing gratitude has proven that you have the potential to rewire the brain and fully eradicate fear in the end. It is through the plasticity cycle that the experiments have shown, with the right behavior and thinking patterns, that you can rewire the brain and remove those nervous causes.

A study conducted by Berkley University showed that, by merely writing gratitude letters or in a gratitude journal, you could improve your mental health in as little as four weeks.

2. GRATITUDE ALLOWS YOU TO SEE PAST YOUR ANXIETY

If you practice appreciation, you can see beyond problems that make you nervous in the first place. Yeah, you may be eager to go to a social gathering, but with your renewed appreciation, you'll pay more attention to the fact that you're seeing people you've missed. The best part of it? It occurs naturally, and the transition in your brain is neither force nor superficial.

3. GRATITUDE HELPS YOU LIVE WELL DESPITE YOUR MENTAL ILLNESS

Gratitude has the potential to boost your well-being. This allows you to live better simply; to be content and satisfied with your life — mentally, emotionally, and physically.

4. GRATITUDE HELPS CREATE TRUST IN THE REDUCTION OF SOCIAL ANXIETY

Several studies have shown that those with appreciation report higher self-esteem levels. This can be of particular benefit to those suffering from a lack of confidence or social anxiety.

5. GRATITUDE ALLOWS YOU TO BE MORE OPTIMISTIC

Feeling positive is a significant part of overcoming fear. After all, when you always see the bad side of things, it may be hard to crawl out of the dark hole.

Fortunately, when gratitude rewires and teaches the brain to see the positive in everything, you naturally become more hopeful. You will see it differently and more optimistic.

Studies have shown that it only takes ten weeks of appreciation activities to witness a drastic increase in motivation.

6. GRATITUDE INCREASES YOUR HAPPINESS

The advantage of appreciation and anxiety goes hand-in-hand with the previous one. If you're more confident, you 're happier.

However, studies have also shown that being happy only makes you happier. A group of researchers performed a report on people sending letters to thank you. For those who have accomplished the mission, there has been a noticeable improvement in happiness and life satisfaction. More significantly, the period of joy and satisfaction lasted for weeks.

7. GRATITUDE ALLEVIATES STRESS

While anxiety and stress are not the same things, they are closely related. Of all, when you're stressed out, it's much easier to get your anxiety activated. Fortunately, appreciation will benefit you.

Evidence has shown that by fostering empathy,

BE GRATEFUL363

you can reduce the levels of cortisol (the stress hormone) by immediately reducing the tension.

8. GRATITUDE HELPS YOU SLEEP AT NIGHT

A lot of anxiety sufferers are unable to get to sleep and sleep because of the racing thoughts in their heads. Loving and feeling thankful will help you with this.

Many studies have shown that it is much easier to get warm, restorative, safe sleep when you're appreciative of the things around you. This is presumably due to the brain rewiring itself and preparing the mind to concentrate on positive things that won't keep you up all night long.

HELPFUL TIPS TO PRACTICING GRATITUDE TO OVERCOME STRESS AND ANXIETY

Being grateful can reduce stress. Can it be that easy? Can being thankful for what you have made you happier?

The following are ten ways in which you can begin to integrate gratitude into your life today:

Using the Gratitude Box - Place two boxes

on your kitchen table-one for grievances and one for stuff you 're grateful for. If you have a complaint about something in your life, write it down and place it in your complaint box. Nevertheless, for each concern, write down the slips of gratitude and place them in the gratitude box. Every day, whether or not you wrote down a question, fill out two slips for a thank you package. Keep it up for at least a month and see if you note that you immediately find some-thing to be thankful for every day instead of seeking a reason to complain.

Develop a Gratitude Journal - Use a customized cover sheet, a notebook, or your phone (there are a variety of gratitude sheet apps) and write down three items that you appreciate every day. Push yourself to do this every day, no matter how you feel about it. Make a promise to write three items every day for 30 days.

Take a Five Minute Break -Take a deep breath and consider what you're grateful for. When you feel stressed out for work, kids, or a fight with your partner, stop what you're doing, sit down, take a few deep breaths (feel your belly full), and relax. Think of three things that make your life worthwhile.

Remember Tough Times from the Past

- You may take your life for granted today, but the chances are that you've been through some difficult times that have influenced the person you are today. Remembering how far you've come, and what you've accomplished will help you know how grateful you need to be for today.

You are using Inspiring Quotations

- Are you having a hard time calming down and talking consciously about what makes you thankful? Some people like to use inspirational quotes as their encouragement to appreciate the world around them. Check online for quotes that suit your situation and take a few moments each day to focus on the quotes you have selected.

Build a Gratitude Board -

Hang a bulletin board in a position that you can see every day. Every day, write down (or share a picture) something you're grateful for or something good in your life. When you post it, look at what you wrote on previous days to remind yourself how happy you are in your life.

Pay Attention to Your Thoughts -

How often are you using derogatory terms or thinking about something or someone in your mind? Pay attention, and when you find yourself doing this, try to turn your thoughts back to something constructive. Hold a notebook with a line drawn down the center of the page if it helps. On the left-hand side, write down your negative feelings. Write a more constructive way to look at the situation on the right.

Stop comparing yourself with others - You often get too short when you compare what you have, how you feel, or something else to others. Remember, you 're not here to catch up with someone else, you 're here to be the best you can be. If you find yourself comparing yourself to someone else, pause and revise your mind to show your gratitude for all the great things that you are!

Practice Mindfulness-The mindfulness is living fully in the present moment. It helps you remain calm and focused. This blocks out the uncertainties of the future or the regrets and heartaches of the past. This reminds you that "this moment" is the most crucial moment and the only one that matters— using relaxation exercises every day to help alleviate tension and to refocus your thoughts.

Tell People Thank You- Gratitude may be the most beautiful gift you may offer to yourself and others. Say "Thank you" to the things you 're thankful for in your life. Let them know if they're talking to you. Not only are you going to make their day, but you 're also going to feel uplifted for expressing your gratitude.

Cultivating gratitude is one of the most natural pathways to a greater sense of mental well-being, higher overall satisfaction in life, and a greater sense of happiness in life. Those with a higher degree of gratitude tend to have better relationships in that they respect their loved ones, and their loved ones, experiencing the appreciation, tend to do more to receive it. And for those who are happier, sleep better, and enjoy good relationships tend to be healthier, grateful people tend to be healthier people.

Fortunately, gratitude can be cultivated, and this can be accomplished in a variety of ways. In the next few weeks, try one of the following activities. You will experience a significant shift in your feelings of gratitude—you will find more positive things in your life, concentrate less on negative or troubling 'lack' thoughts and emotions, and have a stronger sense of appreciation in people and events in your life.

CONCLUSION

Anxiety experience is common and global. It is not an emotion limited to the socially deprived or politically marginalized. Anxiety is an inevitable facet of human experience, and life at all rates, from foreign and organizational to residential and personal, is characterized by confusion, perplexity, and tension. Some persons may want to evade their anxieties, or at least their severity (even on their own) for a multitude of reasons, such as the desire to escape humiliation, the feeling of accomplishment, the dread of rejection, the danger and discomfort of vulnerability, etc., although almost everyone experience anxieties to some measure.

People get nervous and eager and upset from time to time. It is part of human life. In reality, a little bit of concern and anxiety could be a positive thing, because it increases vigilance and notifies us to potential hazards. In that regard, anxiety is natural, and you might find yourself in a lot of trouble if you didn't think about it!

Anxiety becomes an unhealthful condition is when you take hold of your living and turn your way out of control to the point that your sole attention is on the source of your fear. There are different forms of anxiety, and you must have a proper sensitization and diagnosis before any form of treatment should commence. This will make a big difference in the world, and it will decide if you can still minimize or entirely remove excessive anxiety in your life at once. Its presence is upsetting and crippling. That perseverance is debilitating. As long as everyday life is marked by hardship, conflict, and pain, anxiety-experience is inevitable.

Even if we are victims of anxiety, life must still go on. We have to learn how to handle anxiety so that we can continue to survive and prosper. Many people who have anxiety live healthy lives. They have families, work, care, look after children, take holidays, and look like anyone else. The difference is that, at any moment, we can become nervous or suffer from a panic attack. Such attacks can range from total exhaustion to moderate discomfort. Some people are capable of shielding their attacks, so no one with them is the wiser. With some unlucky ones, the fear is so debilitating that it affects their lives and their behaviors, and their behavior is solely dependent on their fear.

Whatever group you might be in, just know that it's possible to function even when you're experiencing anxiety.

Overcoming anxiety as a generalized anxiety disorder will prove to be a problematic activity. Although it is considered standard for individuals to experience some degree of anxiety at one stage or another, it doesn't have to be hard to get rid of anxiety. In truth, it can be surprisingly fast and straightforward. You need to learn the right pieces of knowledge that I'm sure you've learned a lot from this book.

The key to overcoming anxiety starts with education. You need to know what, how, and why, to some degree, treat or cure something. Also, learning something about an anxiety disorder goes a long way towards quenching the symptoms, because you know exactly what you are facing.

Just as mentioned earlier, severally in this guide, overcoming anxiety and panic attacks permanently involve a process that requires much time and dedication. It is essential to understand that it is possible to overcome these problems without using prescription medications permanently.

Anxiety conditions can cause interruptions in your daily life, particularly in your day-to-day interaction and activities. Therefore, managing fear and coping with your fear condition as quickly and effectively is best done to get back to your life before developing an anxiety disorder. Some approaches may help you conquer your anxiety. One of the critical approaches that have been discussed in this guide is self-help strategies. In specific individuals, self-help strategies may be enough to conquer anxiety.

A variety of common self-help approaches to tackle anxiety include the following techniques for restoring our memories: resolving your fears and anxiety in more positive ways-including discussing unreasonable, worrying feelings; learning how to avoid worrying issues, and learning how to accept uncertainty in your life; making the required anxiety-reducing lifestyle changes-including avoiding worrying issues. Learning and practicing relaxation techniques, including deep breathing and meditation.

Knowing how to soothe yourself is another powerful way to conquer fear. Many people who are living with anxiety and depression don't know how to relax and relieve themselves. Mastering how to do this is safe and can make a substantial difference in your ability to handle anxiety. Any or all of the physical senses, the senses of sight, sound, smell, touch, and taste, are the strongest methods of self-soothing.

Sight - Take a look at a magnificent view, have a light stroll in your neighborhood, enjoy art in an art gallery, or take a look at a fascinating picture book.

Sound - Listen to calming songs, love nature's beauty, such as singing birds or sounds of crashing oceans.

Smell - Light flavored candles, inhale flowers outside, breathe in the cold, fresh air, or spray your favorite perfume.

Touch - Pet your cat or dog, take a warm bubble bath, wrap yourself in a soft blanket, feel the cool breeze, or get a massage.

Other natural and self-help methods to overcoming anxiety and related mental disorders include and are not limited to constant exercises such as walking, running, biking, and the likes. Furthermore, self-soothing and self-talks also go a long way towards managing anxiety correctly. Mindfulness meditation and breathing exercises are also sound practices to be taken seriously if an anxiety victim needs to overcome it sooner than later because they both deal with the mind directly.

Finding out time to spend with family, friends, and loved ones is another important factor that helps to deal and conquer anxiety and talk about those worries, challenges, and problems that make us anxious about tomorrow. Pouring those troubles out with a family and friend gives the mind that relief and takes away the burdens off one's mind. Also, as an anxiety sufferer, don't forget to keep up an anti-anxiety diet and avoid too much coffee and caffeine-induced foods and drinks. Last but not least, be always grateful in all conditions you find yourself to maintain a positive attitude against anxiety.

I challenge you to face the head of the monster's anxiety. But in one battle, you may not win the war. It can take a few days, even a few months before you feel enough change to know that you are winning the fight. That's why, right before the war starts, get an out of here. Running out of an anxiety trap never works. You might feel better, but the beast knows it's going to kill you. And every time you meet the beast, you prepare yourself to run. The world looks different. An out is essentially a deal that you made with yourself in the past. You have decided to take a break and return to the situation more stably in the immediate future.

Once again, overcoming anxiety without using medication is a possible task. If you want to experience anxiety relief, naturally, you will need to take control of all of the things that are causing you stress and anxiety.

ABOUT THE AUTHOR

John Ward is a professor, a motivational speaker, an author, and holds two degrees in psychology and neuroscience. He has devoted his life to helping people become their best selves both in the classroom and in countless books.

With his background in behavioral sciences and developmental psychology, John has managed to help numerous people overcome their self-defeating habits in order to become better individuals. He has been a star speaker at self-improvement conferences, local centers for the underprivileged, and sometimes even at college graduations. John wishes to help as many people transform their lives for the better before he himself turns fifty years old.

When he's not writing or teaching, John enjoys traveling the world with his adoring wife of almost twenty years by his side. And because John is a family man, first and foremost, he enjoys spending the free time that he has, with his family. He is proud to father two amazing and successful sons, one of whom, wishes to follow in his father's footsteps and become a motivational speaker himself.

REFERNCES

Phil Barker (7 October 2003). Psychiatric and mental health nursing: the craft of caring. London: Arnold. ISBN 978-0-340-81026-2. Archived from the original on 27 May 2013. Retrieved 17 December 2010.

Psychology, Michael Passer, Ronald Smith, Nigel Holt, Andy Bremner, Ed Sutherland, Michael Vliek (2009) McGrath Hill Education, UK: McGrath Hill Companies Inc. p 790

"All About Anxiety Disorders: From Causes to Treatment and Prevention". Archived from the original on 17 February 2016. Retrieved 18 February 2016.

Psychiatry, Michael Gelder, Richard Mayou,

John Geddes 3rd ed. Oxford; New York: Oxford University Press, c 2005 p. 75

Horney, K. (1917/1968). The technique of psychoanalytic therapy. American Journal of Psychoanalysis, 28, 3-12.

Colton, T, Gossehn, R E., & Smith, R P (1968) The tolerance of coffee drinkers to caffeine Clinical Pharmacology Therapy, 9, 31-39

DeFreitas, B , & Schwartz, G (1979) Effects of caffeine in chronic psychiatric patients American Journal of Psychology. 136, 1337-1338

Goldstein, A, Warren, R, & Kaizer, S (1965). Psychotropic effects of caffeine m man 2 Alertness, psychomotor coordination, and mood Journal of Pharmacology and Experimental Therapeutics, 150, 146-151

Greden, J R, Fontaine, P, Lubetsky, M., & Chamberhn, K (1978) Anxiety and depression associated with caffeinism among psychiatric mpatients American Journal of Psychiatry, 135, 963-966

Horney, K. (1942). Self-analysis. New York: W. W. Norton and Company, Inc.

Horney, K. (1945). Our inner conflicts. New York: Norton. Volume 2. Issue 2. pp 198–199.

Horney, K. (1980). The adolescent diaries of

Karen Horney, 1899-1911. New York: Basic Books. pp 499

Hornstein, G. A. (1992). The return of the repressed: Psychology's problematic relations with psychoanalys, 1909-1960. American Psychologist., 47, 254-263.

Marzola, L. (2009). Karen Horney Basic Anxiety. Psychology Helium.

O'Connell, A. N. (1990). Karen Horney (1885-1952). Women in psychology: A bio-bibliographic sourcebook, (pp. 184–190). Westport, CT: Greenwood Press.

Schultz, D., Schultz S. (2012). A History of Modern Psychology. Wadsworth Cengage Learning.

Varcarolis. E (2010). Manual of Psychiatric Nursing Care Planning: Assessment Guides, Diagnoses and Psychopharmacology. 4th ed. New York: Saunders Elsevier. p 109.

Keeton, CP; Kolos, AC; Walkup, JT (2009). "Pediatric generalized anxiety disorder: epidemiology, diagnosis, and management". Paediatric Drugs. 11 (3): 171–83. doi:10.2165/00148581-200911030-00003. PMID 19445546.

"Panic Disorder". Center for the Treatment

and Study of Anxiety, University of Pennsylvania. Archived from the original on 27 May 2015.

Colton, T, Gossehn, R E., & Smith, R P (1968) The tolerance of coffee drinkers to caffeine Clinical Pharmacology Therapy, 9, 31-39

DeFreitas, B , & Schwartz, G (1979) Effects of caffeine in chronic psychiatric patients American Journal of Psychology. 136, 1337-1338

Goldstein, A, Warren, R, & Kaizer, S (1965). Psychotropic effects of caffeine m man 2 Alertness, psychomotor coordination, and mood Journal of Pharmacology and Experimental Therapeutics, 150, 146-151

Greden, J R, Fontaine, P, Lubetsky, M., & Chamberhn, K (1978) Anxiety and depression associated with caffeinism among psychiatric mpatients American Journal of Psychiatry, 135, 963-966

Hire, J N (1978) Anxiety and caffeine Psychological Reports, 42, 833-834

Klemfeld, C (1977) Handbook of nonprescnptwn drugs

U.S. Department of Health & Human Services (2017). "Phobias". www.mentalhealth.gov. Archived from the original on 13 May 2017. Retrieved 1 December 2017.

Addicott, MA (2014). "Caffeine Use Disorder: A Review of the Evidence and Future Implications". Current Addiction Reports. 1 (3): 186–192. doi:10.1007/s40429-014-0024-9. PMC 4115451. PMID 25089257.

Hughes, R.N. (June 1996). "Drugs Which Induce Anxiety: Caffeine" (PDF). 25. New Zealand Journal of Psychology. Archived from the original (PDF) on 2020-01-30.

Winston, Anthony P.; Hardwick, Elizabeth; Jaberi, Neema (October 2005). "Neuropsychiatric effects of caffeine". Advances in Psychiatric Treatment. 11 (6): 432–439. doi:10.1192/apt.11.6.432. ISSN 2056-4678.

American Psychiatric Association (2013). Diagnostic and Statistical Manual of Mental Disorders (DSM-5). American Psychiatric Publishing. pp. 226–230. ISBN 978-0-89042-555-8.

Torres, Francis M. (April 2009). "Caffeine - Induced Psychiatric Disorders" (PDF). Journal of Continuing Education Topics & Issues. Retrieved 22 February 2016.

Yang, Amy; Palmer, Abraham A.; de Wit, Harriet (June 9, 2010). "Genetics of caffeine

consumption and responses to caffeine".
Psychopharmacology. 2 1 1 (3): 245–257.

Psychology. Michael Passer, Ronald Smith,
Nigel Holt, Andy Bremner, Ed Sutherland,
Michael Vliek. (2009) McGrath Hill Higher
Education; UK: McGrath Hill companies Inc.

(5th ed) Washington, DC American Phar-
maceutical Association Kozlowski, L T (1976).
Effect of caffeine on coffee drinking Nature, 264,
354-355 Kulhanek, F , Lmde, O I, & Meisenberg, G
(1979, Nov 24) Precipitation of antipsychotic
drugs m interaction with coffee or tea Lancet, 1 1 3 0

Truitt, E B (1971) The xanthines In J R Dipalma
(Ed), Drill's pharmacology in medicine (4th ed)
New York McGraw-Hill Winstead, B (1976)
Coffee consumption among psychiatric mpatients
American Journal of Psychiatry, 133, 1447-1450

Zuckerman, M , Lubm, B, Vogel, L., &
Valenous, E (1964) Measurement of experimen-
tally induced affects Journal of Consulting
Psychology, 28, 418-425

Printed in Great Britain
by Amazon

36396121R00220